RESEARCH RECOMMENDATIONS

TO FACILITATE
DISTRIBUTED
WORK

Technology and Telecommuting: Issues and Impacts Committee
Computer Science and Telecommunications Board
Commission on Physical Sciences, Mathematics, and Applications
National Research Council

NATIONAL ACADEMY PRESS
Washington, D.C. 1994

Support for this project was provided by the Department of Energy (Grant No. DE-FG02-93ER25161), and that support does not constitute an endorsement by the Department of Energy of the views expressed in the report.

Library of Congress Catalog Card Number 94-68990

International Standard Book Number 0-309-05185-1

Additional copies of this report are available from:

National Academy Press
2101 Constitution Avenue, NW
Box 285
Washington, DC 20055

800-624-6242
202-334-3313
(in the Washington metropolitan area)

B-498

Printed in the United States of America

TECHNOLOGY AND TELECOMMUTING:
ISSUES AND IMPACTS COMMITTEE

The National Academy of Sciences is a private, nonprofit, self-perpetuating society of distinguished scholars engaged in scientific and engineering research, dedicated to the furtherance of science and technology and to their use for the general welfare. Upon the authority of the charter granted to it by Congress in 1863, the Academy has a mandate that requires it to advise the federal government on scientific and technical matters. Dr. Bruce Alberts is president of the National Academy of Sciences.

The National Academy of Engineering was established in 1964, under the charter of the National Academy of Sciences, as a parallel organization of outstanding engineers. It is autonomous in its administration and in the selection of its members, sharing with the National Academy of Sciences the responsibility for advising the federal government. The National Academy of Engineering also sponsors engineering programs aimed at meeting national needs, encourages education and research, and recognizes the superior achievements of engineers. Dr. Robert M. White is president of the National Academy of Engineering.

The Institute of Medicine was established in 1970 by the National Academy of Sciences to secure the services of eminent members of appropriate professions in the examination of policy matters pertaining to the health of the public. The Institute acts under the responsibility given to the National Academy of Sciences by its congressional charter to be an adviser to the federal government and, upon its own initiative, to identify issues of medical care, research, and education. Dr. Kenneth I. Shine is president of the Institute of Medicine.

The National Research Council was organized by the National Academy of Sciences in 1916 to associate the broad community of science and technology with the Academy's purposes of furthering knowledge and advising the federal government. Functioning in accordance with general policies determined by the Academy, the Council has become the principal operating agency of both the National Academy of Sciences and the National Academy of Engineering in providing services to the government, the public, and the scientific and engineering communities. The Council is administered jointly by both Academies and the Institute of Medicine. Dr. Bruce Alberts and Dr. Robert M. White are chairman and vice chairman, respectively, of the National Research Council.

Preface

In 1993, the Department of Energy (DOE) asked the Computer Science and Telecommunications Board (CSTB) of the National Research Council to organize a study of the technological issues and impacts related to telecommuting. In response, CSTB, in collaboration with the NRC's Transportation Research Board (TRB), convened a committee of researchers and practitioners with both technical and sociological expertise. The committee's task was to recommend research into relevant computing and communications technologies that could enable increased telecommuting. In developing these recommendations the committee relied on existing literature, briefings, and its own expertise and deliberations. With the agreement of DOE, the study committee chose to broaden its approach to its task in two specific ways. First, it chose to examine both telecommuting and the broader topic of distributed work, because it believed that focusing solely on telecommuting would overlook more far-reaching impacts of computing and telecommunications technology on the way work is done. Second, the committee chose to examine technological issues within a broad social context in order to ensure the relevance of its recommendations.

This study is the result of the study committee's deliberations. It is independent of and complementary to the April 1993 Department of Transportation study, *Transportation Implications of Telecommuting*

(U.S. Government Printing Office, Washington, D.C.), on the future impacts of telecommuting on transportation, and to the DOE study *Energy, Emissions, and Social Consequences of Telecommuting* (U.S. Government Printing Office, Washington, D.C.), which was released in early 1994. The publication of *Research Recommendations to Facilitate Distributed Work* during 1994 will allow its conclusions and recommendations to be considered during the development of the National Information Infrastructure (NII) in the same manner as those regarding other nationally important applications such as education and health care.

At another level, the committee is convinced that computing, telecommunications, and related technologies are profoundly changing the ways in which society acquires, manages, and distributes information. In the private sector, the development of new tools for distributed work could enable new forms of collaboration, allowing employees to work effectively at any location that is mutually agreeable to them and their employers. One result could be new, more productive configurations of people, processes, and technology. In the public sector, new tools for distributed work could be used to address high-priority needs, such as rural and inner-city health care, and to remedy long-standing inequities among the nation's classrooms.

A nationwide information and network infrastructure could open new avenues for mutual cooperation and support among our workplaces, schools, neighborhood centers, community groups, and government. This new digital environment has the potential to enable a richness in information access and sharing that could help us restore a sense of community within and between the public and private sectors. Achieving such goals will depend on having both the specific knowledge and broad understanding needed to implement appropriate technology wisely. In accordance with that concept, this report complements two other recent CSTB reports, *Information Technology in the Service Society* and *Realizing the Information Future* (both published by National Academy Press, Washington, D.C., 1994), and the forthcoming *Rights and Responsibilities of Participants in Networked Communities.*

The Technology and Telecommuting: Issues and Impacts Committee is grateful to the numerous individuals who contributed to its deliberations and to those who commented on early drafts of this report. The anonymous reviewers in particular helped to sharpen and focus the material. The staff of the Computer Science and Telecommunications Board and the Transportation Research Board were indispensable in creating the report. Gloria Bemah attended to the

multitude of details required for committee meetings and report production, Leslie Wade helped check references, and Jim Mallory trans-
formed the committee's submissions into the final text. The committee, however, retains responsibility for the final content of the report.

Robert Kraut, *Chair*
Technology and Telecommuting:
Issues and Impacts Committee

Contents

Executive Summary

The term "distributed work" describes the practice of working without regard to location by using a combination of modern communications and computing technologies. It includes:

- Working while truly mobile—in activities ranging from sales and on-site customer support or equipment repair to composing and submitting a product design while traveling;
- Working as part of a geographically dispersed project team— in activities such as research and report writing done largely without traveling to a common site; and
- Traditional telecommuting—carrying out activities such as responding to customers' telephone calls by utilizing a personal computer linked to a remote database while working at home or at a satellite work center.

Distributed workers can engage in these activities on a full-time basis, as might be the case for a distributed customer service operation. Perhaps more commonly, however, they may engage in the practice of distributed work on a part-time basis, such as spending a day per week contributing to a company-wide product evaluation.

To the extent that a job involves or is enhanced by the creation, manipulation, storage, or communication of information, it is increasingly possible to do that job anywhere that the appropriate information processing equipment and communications links are found. There are numerous economic and social benefits to be gained by enhancing and extending distributed work practices. These include increased locational independence for employees, greater flexibility in convening project teams for employers, and better use of transportation resources for society. There are also some potential disadvantages, such as loss of contact and identification with an organization, as well as a possible increase in demands on employees' time and energy. Although many individuals already engage in distributed work, current technologies have several important limitations, especially for groups whose members are geographically dispersed and for individuals who need to work while truly mobile. However, technology itself is only an enabler of or constraint on change rather than a direct motivator of change. Thus, along with better technologies, distributed work practices will also be enhanced by a better understanding of the human factors and sociology of the changing workplace and labor force.

Recent improvements in the capabilities and availability of communications and computing tools have meant that distributed work, including telecommuting, can be done more easily now than in the past. Likewise, future improvements in these interrelated fields will benefit those engaged in distributed work. However, to optimize the opportunities for and effectiveness of distributed work, the study committee recommends that research also be conducted with distributed work as a specific focus.

RESEARCH RECOMMENDATIONS

Computing power, in terms of processing speed and mass storage capacity, and communication capabilities, in terms of available bandwidth and quality of services, can be viewed as a spectrum of varying capacities. Currently, with respect to distributed work, the "high end" of the spectrum may be thought of as being represented by a fully configured desktop workstation attached to a high-bandwidth network. The "low end" of the spectrum may be considered to be characterized by a small hand-held device such as a personal digital assistant with only low-bandwidth wireless communications capabilities.

Through the middle part of the capability spectrum, the nation's computing and communications infrastructure is reasonably well established and utilized. High-speed modems and communications services are decreasing in price and becoming more widely used. Both individuals and organizations have abundant computing power readily available, and the most pressing need is for applications re-search. Conversely, the communications and computing communi-ties should conduct research aimed at stretching the capabilities of the network and computing infrastructure at both the low and high end of the spectrum. The committee's recommendations for techni-cal research are detailed in Chapter 5 of the report and summarized below.

Infrastructure Research

Working while mobile presents many challenges, because com-munications bandwidth and computing power are limited compared to what is typically available in a stationary environment with a wire or optical fiber network connection. The committee's research rec-ommendations center on increasing the bandwidth available to mo-bile workers and better using whatever bandwidth is available at any point in time, as well as facilitating periods of disconnected work when there is no bandwidth at all. The fact that communications bandwidth and computing power can often be substituted for each other both complicates and adds promise to research at the low end of the capability spectrum.

Research at the high end of the infrastructure capability spec-trum should center on exploring distributed work practices that can be facilitated by multipoint, multimedia communication at generally abundant bandwidths. Currently, little is known about transmitting large volumes of interactive, multimedia traffic among multiple par-ties. The committee recommends research centered on understand-ing and specifying quality-of-service factors, controlling the various types of traffic, enabling new billing methods, and minimizing the human efforts currently involved in establishing and maintaining multipoint, multimedia conference sessions.

Applications Research

Various types of distributed work are reasonably common in the U.S. workplace. However, the implementation and effectiveness of distributed work are often constrained by the computing and com-munications applications available to support it. The committee rec-ommends research-oriented distributed work field trials in areas of national or commercial interest to help solve the difficult problems of information retrieval, sharing, and browsing; group socialization; re-mote supervision; and related problems in the context of real-world employer-employee distributed work relationships. While these field trials would be conducted within specific domains, the lessons learned and tools developed could be applied in many other fields as well. An interdisciplinary approach is needed to gain the full benefit of such trials.

The committee also recommends more general research related to applications to benefit telecommuting. If distributed work is to expand beyond those individuals with considerable technical skill, researchers must pay attention to simplifying complex user interfaces and commonly required operations. Research should concentrate on developing tools, interfaces, and systems that encourage information sharing; bridging synchronous and asynchronous communications to facilitate input to and follow-up from group work sessions; improving and extending the user interface to the telephone network and services; improving capabilities to use audio as a data type; and reducing the costs of input/output devices and network support.

CONCLUSION

During a period when the nation's economy seems to be in transition to a postindustrial model, the nation and its work force would be well served by having efficient and effective tools for engaging in distributed work. The research topics addressed by the committee in Chapter 5 will provide important new technological capabilities to enhance and extend the practice of distributed work to provide greater locational flexibility, expanded employment opportunities, and better use of our transportation resources.

1

Technology and the Changing Workplace

NEW OPPORTUNITIES FOR FLEXIBLE WORK

To the extent that a job involves or is enhanced by the creation, manipulation, storage, or communication of information, it is increasingly possible to do that job anywhere that the appropriate information processing equipment and telecommunications links are found. This is true not only for jobs performed by a single isolated individual, but also for group tasks, such as decision making, that involve multiple individuals in dispersed locations.

There are many potential benefits of the flexibility that locational independence provides. For an employer, those benefits may include the ability to recruit the best workers anywhere without requiring them to move to a central location, the ability to assemble and disassemble teams on an as-needed basis, the ability to offer improved customer service through coverage over longer hours and a greater geographical area, and savings in overhead costs through more efficient use of space. For a worker, the benefits of locational independence may include a more desirable lifestyle: greater choice in residential location, type of job, and allocation of time between work and personal interests. For society, benefits may include greater economic efficiency, opportunities for economic development in underdeveloped areas, expanded employment opportunities for individuals with limited mobility, and more efficient use of the transportation infrastructure.

However, the potential benefits of greater flexibility in where and when work can be done must be balanced against the potential costs or disadvantages. For an employer, disadvantages may include the direct costs of investing in the requisite technology, the intangible costs of learning how to use new tools and develop new styles of management suited to distributed work, less opportunity for certain kinds of serendipitous productivity (e.g., clearing up of a misunderstanding during a chance meeting at the coffee pot), and some loss of distributed workers' identification with an organization. For a worker, disadvantages may include loss of privacy, the blurring of boundaries between work and personal activities, fewer chances to interact socially with colleagues, and the increasing domination of work over other aspects of life if the worker is expected to be constantly on call for the employer. Employees may bear part of the costs of a new distributed work style if, for example, the employer allows telecommuting only by those who are willing to provide their own computers. Loss of job security and fringe benefits can result from any shift toward a greater use of temporary and contract workers and the flattening of organizational hierarchies. Increased social isolation may be a negative outcome for some distributed workers.

For society, a negative consequence of greater flexibility may be a fragmented populace that is increasingly able to segregate itself into homogeneous strata. The ability to enjoy a distributed work style may be inequitably distributed, and the socioeconomic gap between the information "haves" and "have nots" may continue to widen. The off-shore relocation of some location-independent work, increased automation of jobs, and associated organizational restructuring may contribute to increased domestic unemployment (CSTB, 1994a). Finally, greater flexibility for workers in choosing where to live may further exacerbate urban sprawl and result in too-rapid growth in rural areas. (See the report *Energy, Emissions, and Social Consequences of Telecommuting* (U.S. Department of Energy, 1994) for detailed discussion of many of the societal impacts of telecommuting.)

Until recently, the information technology that was commonly available, the communications infrastructure, and prevailing work practices have inhibited individuals and organizations from taking full advantage of the potential benefits of flexibility in the place and time of work. For example, when 300-baud modems were the norm, each full computer screen of text took approximately 50 seconds to transfer, and most file transfers had to be manually initiated at both the origin and destination. Increasingly, however, the proliferation of more affordable, more portable, more powerful, and somewhat easier to use computing systems and telecommunications equipment has broadened the opportunities for effective, efficient location-independent work. Developments on the horizon, such as greater integration of information, communications, and multimedia systems, suggest that these opportunities will continue to expand. Simultaneously, on the demand side, changes in the economy, increased time pressures, a desire to reduce energy consumption, corporate layoffs, and the growing use of work teams have resulted in increased interest in implementing telecommuting and distributed work programs and projects.

Together, the new enabling technologies and an increase in demand are likely to result in an increase in location-independent work. How such work can best be facilitated and integrated to meet individual, group, and national needs and expectations is a topic that merits careful study.

THIS REPORT

Approach and Emphasis

Despite the growing interest in and potential benefits of distributed work, there are many technological, economic, and social barriers to its wider adoption. Although in its deliberations the committee focused initially on developing a technical research agenda, it quickly realized the importance of acknowledging context. Distributed work is an area for which consideration of purely technical issues is potentially misleading and counterproductive. Thus, in addition to outlining goals for technological research that could facilitate wider adoption of distributed work among individuals and organizations, this report also emphasizes the need to understand the broader social, economic, and public policy impacts of wider use of computing and communications technology, including possible negative impacts and how to ameliorate them. Although detailed treatment of such issues is outside the direct charge to the committee, social and economic considerations—e.g., the capability for ubiquity of connection, or the willingness and ability of people to work independently and often in relative isolation—provide the larger framework within which specific technical decisions are made and directions taken. The committee concluded that understanding that framework is an essential precondition to making the most effective technical decisions. The results of such decisions will be seen in the long-term ability of comparatively new activities like distributed work to contribute positively to U.S. national life.

Scope and Definitions—
Telecommuting Versus Distributed Work

One difficulty in discussing new work styles is the widespread lack of consensus on the use of terms such as "telecommuting" and "teleworking" (see Kraut, 1988, for one discussion of the difficulties associated with defining and measuring the amount of telecommuting). It has been suggested (Mokhtarian, 1991a) that two factors that distinguish telecommuting from other forms of remote work are remote supervision and a reduction in commuting. Under these criteria, overtime work done at home in the evening by an insurance company executive, for example, would generally not be considered telecommuting because it does not involve a reduction in travel. In contrast, an employee of a software publisher who answers telephone requests for technical assistance from his or her home, instead of answering the questions while present at a centrally located help-line location, is certainly engaged in telecommuting. Likewise, a person doing transcription for a medical clinic and submitting the completed work via a modem and telephone line is a telecommuter.

However, to focus exclusively on telecommuting, as narrowly defined, is to overlook the sweeping nature of technology-supported changes that are affecting virtually every employer and every worker. These changes are leading to a work style that may be broadly referred to as distributed work: work that is done in a location different from that of the supervisor, subordinate, or fellow team member. Distributed work includes mobile work (work done while traveling), computer-supported cooperative work, field work, off-shore information processing, teleconferencing, and numerous other arrangements as well as home- and center-based telecommuting. To encompass the diversity of current approaches to location-independent work and to develop a correspondingly broad research agenda, this report examines distributed work of various kinds in an effort to delineate the strengths and limitations of current computing and communications technologies for enabling effective work.

TECHNOLOGY AND SOCIETY

It is important to view technology in its proper role as an enabler of, or constraint on, change, rather than as the direct motivator of social or individual change. An individual may be motivated to telecommute not because technology permits it, but rather, for example, to avoid an onerous commute, to get more work done, or to have more time to spend with family. An employer may be motivated to adopt telecommuting for its staff not because technology makes it possible, but rather to improve recruitment and retention, save money, increase productivity, or help comply with mandated trip-reduction goals. Confusing an enabler of change with a motivation for change is likely to lead to overstating the potential impacts of the enabler, which does not alone guarantee that change will occur. Change will occur when there are no binding constraints and when one or more motivations are present (Mokhtarian and Salomon, 1994).

New technologies sometimes emerge because they are needed; that is, researchers are motivated to develop a technology because they are aware of a need that the technology can satisfy. Often, there is a cyclical interrelationship between technological and social issues related to the work environment: the social context gives rise to the need for a given technology, and over time, that technology may have social impacts that are significant enough to alter the social context, giving rise to the need for another round of technological innovation. For example, Yates (1989) has shown that as corporations grew and organized into divisions, the internal office memorandum was developed to increase communications and document organizational procedures. Typewriters, filing systems, various copying technologies, and word processors were all developed to meet the demand for more memoranda and other written materials. More recently, electronic mail was developed to meet a variety of immediate communication needs in an increasingly distributed environment. Each of these technologies affected society by creating new classes of jobs, which in turn often led to further organizational division and the resultant need for even newer, better forms of communication.

In other instances, technological research is driven by the desire to expand knowledge and capabilities for their own sake, without consideration for their likely application. Research and development conducted without specific needs in mind may produce important scientific understanding, new technologies, and solutions to problems that are not yet widely recognized. However, research that is exclusively technology-driven also may produce solutions that no one wants and for which there is no market, or solutions that some may even view as potentially damaging.

The social context of research efforts helps ensure that some of each type of research is conducted. Generally, exploration of technology for its own sake is balanced by economic and social realities, and pragmatism is balanced by opportunities for unexpected discoveries. Regardless of the motivation, new technologies may permit us not only to do the old things better, but also to do new things that are not imagined until the enabling technology is available. The practice of distributed work and the technologies developed to support it are best examined in relation to society and with an understanding that they will have important impacts on all of us.

The Rise of Distributed Work— Representative Concerns

Impacts on Transportation and Land Use

Telecommuting per se is frequently proposed as a strategy for reducing peak-period vehicle trips, fuel consumption, and air pollution by substituting communications for travel. It has been included as such in a variety of federal, state, and regional or local policy statements (see, e.g., Mokhtarian, 1991b). A great deal of research has been conducted on the transportation-related impacts of telecommuting. Some of the early studies hypothesized about the ultimate extent of telecommuting and its effects on transportation (for a review, see, e.g., Salomon, 1986). It was suggested, for example, that the travel mileage saved by telecommuting might be partially or completely offset by an increase in noncommuting trips motivated by some inherent desire for mobility or travel. Empirically, this effect of generating more travel has not been found to date. The measured net impact of telecommuting on transportation has been a relatively uniform reduction in miles traveled: an average of 36.1 person-miles saved per telecommuting occurrence (Mokhtarian et al., 1994). However, these findings are based on short-term studies involving small samples of early adopters of telecommuting who may be unrepresentative of the population that eventually engages in it. For example, studies published to date have found that telecommuters live about twice as far from work as the average commuter in their region. As telecommuting moves into the mainstream, the per capita travel savings of telecommuting is likely to decline but will probably remain positive on balance.

A broader critical issue concerns the transportation-related impacts of enhanced computing and telecommunications capabilities generally, not just those of telecommuting. What will be the impacts on transportation of distributed work activities such as the remote acquisition of goods and services, tele- and videoconferencing, product or project coordination with business partners, and consumer activities such as teleshopping? There are a few isolated empirical and anecdotal examples of complementary effects (Mokhtarian, 1988, 1990), such as electronic access to information and people prompting travel to obtain further information or to develop a relationship, or a regional videoconference stimulating travel because it is accessible to more people than would be a single national conference without video. However, such complementary impacts of distributed work activities on transportation have not been studied as extensively as substitution and generation impacts. Thus the possibility of distributed work leading to more employment-related travel remains a fertile area for research.

Another important social impact of using computing and telecommunications technology for distributed work involves changes in land use patterns. A commonly held hypothesis is that distributed work will make it possible for people to move even farther from central sites than they currently live, possibly leading to a net increase in travel. Again, the empirical evidence to date (Nilles, 1991; Mokhtarian, 1994) has not borne out the hypothesis that distributed work will lead to fewer but longer commuting trips in the aggregate, although no long-term evaluation has been made. A simple theoretical model based on economic location theory (Lund and Mokhtarian, 1994) suggests that even after optimal residential relocation occurs, total commute-miles traveled will generally be lower because of more widespread telecommuting, but more research is needed to refine such a model and to test it empirically.

In the literature on the general impacts of computing and telecommunications on land use and urban form, the most commonly expressed expectation is that their use will lead to greater decentralization. However, it is also pointed out that telecommunications is usually a facilitator, not a driver, of decisions about residential and industrial location and that it can support centralization as well as decentralization. For example, although the elevator is considered to have made modern skyscrapers possible, the telephone played an equally important role in making them practical (de Sola Pool, 1980). Although computing and telecommunications may support a relative decline in the advantage of central locations, these locations will retain a competitive advantage due to the economics of agglomeration and the existence of their massive, already-built environments (Nijkamp and Salomon, 1989).

Social Isolation

One reason for early skepticism about the widespread adoption of telecommuting was the idea that people would not want to be isolated from others. The assumption seemed to be that telecommuting was to be full-time work from home. Current experience indicates that telecommuting is most often part-time: one or two days per week on average. At this level, isolation and related issues such as visibility to management are not often cited as concerns by telecommuters. However, there is obviously some self-selection bias in considering the responses only of telecommuters, while not obtaining and considering the responses of those who may have chosen not to telecommute because of the possibility of isolation. Even when telecommuting is virtually full-time, telecommuters and, for that matter, millions of home-based business owners have found numerous strategies for circumventing isolation (Christensen, 1988; Race, 1993; Shellenbarger, 1993). These strategies include participating in local chapters of professional organizations, having lunch with colleagues, and using electronic mail extensively. Thus, the same technology that permits increased isolation can also be used to decrease it. Finally, experimentation with telecommuting at satellite work centers like the federal telecommuting center in Waldorf, Maryland, is increasing (Bagley et al., 1993). One hypothesized advantage of such centers is that they offer an opportunity for some social and perhaps professional interaction.

The effects of isolation may reach beyond the individual actively engaged in telecommuting. For example, individuals who become isolated as the result of corporate downsizing (a department of specialists may be reduced to a single individual) may require contacts with other human beings (i.e., networks) in other organizations to survive in their jobs. In such cases, too, distributed work technologies can decrease isolation as well as cause it: electronic mail, computer-aided conferencing, and the on-line availability of conference proceedings can help individuals to keep current within their occupations.

A broader question concerns the impact of computing and telecommunications in general on social isolation. Arguably, these technologies, much like television, have contributed to social isolation, although just as arguably, they have also given rise to new forms and norms of socialization. Technology is a tool that can be used to break down social barriers by enabling egalitarian access through such mechanisms as electronic mail communications, as much as it can be used to facilitate separation through mechanisms such as the increased opportunity to choose isolated residential locations.

Management and Personnel Considerations

The process of selecting personnel for telecommuting can be usefully represented as a triangle: the right employees, jobs, and managers must be selected to ensure the success of telecommuting. More than 10 years of practical experience have helped define the selection criteria for each. Most important is the selection of remote workers, which should be based on a combination of well-informed volunteerism from the employees and final selection by management, based on the employees' work habits, skills, and knowledge of the organization.

Supervision of remote workers has been the primary stumbling block for many organizations considering telecommuting. The perennial question is, How can I tell they're working when they're not here in the office? The best answer is brought out by another question, How can you tell they're working when they are here in the office? This exchange highlights the fact that many managers practice "eyeball management," often erroneously assuming that if work and workers can be seen, workers are working and being supervised. Effective managers of telecommuters learn that it is the product, not the presence of a person or a visible process, that counts; they should be selected and trained so that they are comfortable managing workers according to the end product produced. Likewise, jobs that have, or can be modified to have, ascertainable end products and quantifiable standards for quality should be considered as the prime candidates for distributed work.

Managing or working successfully to produce expected deliverables means that telecommuters are relatively free to work how and when they want as long as the end product meets expectations. Conversely, managers and workers who prefer command-and-control organizational styles may find it uncomfortable, if not impossible, to manage and work at a distance. Thus, in the short term, the perceived loss of control of remote workers is a concern that could inhibit more widespread implementation of distributed work practices.

Other Impacts and Public Policy Considerations

Beyond concerns about effectiveness, efficiency, social consequences, management, and personnel issues that will be resolved largely on a case-by-case basis are a number of broad public policy issues associated with the expansion of distributed work. They will need to be discussed, understood, and addressed in order for distributed work to expand to the fullest extent possible. Perhaps foremost is the question of the amount of private and public support for the infrastructure that is likely to be needed to provide the enhanced communications services required for distributed work. In the past, the nation has supported infrastructure development by providing general or limited monopolies, loans, grants, construction subsidies, and tax incentives. In most recent developments involving technology, however, the private sector has been the main investor in new facilities. Given the broad range of technological capabilities that may be needed for distributed work, it seems likely that private funding will play the major role, with government supplementing efforts only in areas that will not be addressed without such assistance. User fees and access to new services are also a concern to many, particularly to those who believe that access to information and communications over the National Information Infrastructure will be necessary to fully participate in tomorrow's society and economy.

Financial considerations will also affect our ability as a nation to further develop and expand our capabilities for distributed work. Although since World War II the federal government has played a crucial role in financing both basic and applied research in numerous fields, that role is now in transition, and there is great uncertainty regarding the philosophy for support and levels of federal funding for various fields.

The increased practice of distributed work also raises concerns about intellectual property rights, privacy, and the security of information as it is stored, accessed, and processed electronically. Several reports of the National Research Council have detailed these issues. *Computers at Risk* (CSTB, 1990), *Realizing the Information Future* (CSTB, 1994b), and *Rights and Responsibilities of Participants in Networked Communities* (CSTB, 1994c) are helpful for their discussion and recommendations on these and related issues.

SUMMARY COMMENTS

The overall societal consequences of distributed work practices are not yet completely clear, and their treatment is not within the scope of this study. Many researchers in academia, industry, and government are currently examining distributed work, including telecommuting, in order to gain a better understanding of its advantages and disadvantages. A recent Department of Energy report, *Energy, Emissions, and Social Consequences of Telecommuting* (U.S. Department of Energy, 1994), summarizes much of this research, and the Department of Transportation's *Transportation Implications of Telecommuting* (U.S. Department of Transportation, 1993) focuses more detailed scrutiny on transportation. *Intellectual Teamwork: Social and Technological Foundations of Cooperative Work* (Kraut et al., 1990) is also useful for its linking of social and work issues and technology. The committee underscores the need for open and detailed discussion of the public policies that may be implemented with respect to the practice of distributed work. Technology and society have a complex relationship that is constantly changing (see, e.g., CSTB, 1994a). It will be important for researchers to address not only the technical agenda recommended in this report, but also interrelated social and economic issues.

2

Distributed Work:
Current Reality and Promise

This chapter describes today's distributed work landscape, exploring current uses, benefits, limitations, potential enhancements, and opportunities for expansion. Its purpose is not to describe an exhaustive set of applications and scenarios, but rather to aid in exploring the need for further technological research aimed at enhancing distributed work. Although the initial discussion focuses on the representative activities of information processing and communicating at various levels, it is clear that jobs vary in the extent to which they require complex handling of data, people, and things (see U.S. Department of Labor, 1991). Dealing with people and objects requires tools that are different from those for dealing with information. U.S. industry has developed a rich palette of mail and telecommunications applications to enable communication among people at a distance. However, even in regular telephone communications, improvement is needed for some typical distributed work tasks. In comparison, there are even fewer techniques for dealing with objects at a distance.

ASPECTS OF DISTRIBUTED WORK
ENABLED BY COMPUTING AND
COMMUNICATIONS TECHNOLOGY

The last 15 years have seen a proliferation of information technologies and communications applications that let people do their work while overcoming some of the limitations of space and time. Corporate databases, electronic libraries, and information servers help people retrieve, process, and store the information they need to do their jobs, regardless of location. Facsimile, electronic mail, and audio- and videoconferencing now routinely supplement long-standing communications media such as face-to-face meetings, postal mail, and the telephone, keeping people in touch with their fellow employees and with their clients and customers. The traditional media also have changed: many telephone systems now include voice mail, the U.S. Postal Service offers overnight delivery, and formerly widespread telex service has been largely replaced by other communications technologies. Home-based resources, too, have been augmented: national surveys have shown that doing paid employment from the home is the best predictor of having a computer at home (Dudley et al., 1993).

Information Processing

Declines in the cost of computing hardware and the concomitant growth in the use of computers for both routine and strategic purposes in organizations mean that much of the information that people need to do their jobs is in computerized form at some point during its life cycle. And once information is in computerized form, it becomes possible for people to access it with comparatively few logistical constraints on where they are and when they do so. Much of the information available to remote personnel is generated as a by-product of an organization's routine transaction processing, rather than created specifically for the purpose of supporting distributed work. For example, computerized reservation systems for the airline industry were developed to allow a highly distributed work force of travel agents to gain up-to-date information about flight schedules and prices. A variant of this reservation system combined with nationwide data networks such as CompuServe now allows average citizens to access the same information on their personal computers at home. Similarly, by using database technology combined with call distributors and other telecommunications services, some customer service representatives are able to do their work independent of location. Service representatives working for a telephone company, for example, can access recent bills, customer credit history, and databases of help information so that they can resolve billing conflicts, collect past-due accounts, take new service orders, and answer customer questions.

Many workers can also have at their disposal information beyond that created by a single organization. For a fee, individuals and firms can access any of the thousands of commercial databases containing a vast array of information, including the full text of legal cases; financial information about firms from various sources, including Securities and Exchange Commission filings; consumer and business credit information; patent filings; stock quotations; the full text of national and regional newspapers; and research articles in virtually every scientific and technical field. An increasing number of databases (especially for government-generated or government-owned information) are also becoming available on a no-fee basis via the Internet.

Moreover, recent developments in information publishing and retrieval have made increasing amounts of information available on public networks such as the Internet and America OnLine. For example, a tool developed by researchers at CERN in Geneva, the World-Wide Web, links documents and files connected by the Internet. The information in the Web is based on a hyper-text mark-up language protocol that makes it possible for individuals and organizations to publish information on the Internet that is cross-linked both internally and to external documents. For example, selecting, or clicking on, a highlighted word within a document can initiate retrieval of its definition, or related information, from within that same document, or even from a document at another location on the network. This capability allows the user to browse easily through related pieces of information, or groups of related documents, without regard to the physical location of the information. This and other new techniques for information retrieval on computer networks (including the easy-to-use Mosaic interface to the World-Wide Web) have stimulated the supply of available information by improving access to it, but they have also led to increased network traffic.

Taken together, the availability of company and other databases, commercial database services, and the networks that connect them mean that many people can be much less reliant on centralized, physically co-located corporate resources to do their jobs. Lawyers do not need the corporate law library if an electronic library is available, and service representatives need not be tied to file cabinets of paper invoices. It is clear that people use electronic archives of information when they work away from a conventional work site.

Yet there are practical limits on the extent to which people can work away from a conventional work site, remote from peers and supervisors, merely by relying on electronic archives. The major consideration is the availability in electronic form of the information people need to perform information-intensive tasks. Sales representatives for mail-order companies have in electronic form most of the information they need to take an order—product and inventory information, for example. Yet other information that they might need to aid a customer, such as the exact color of a product and whether it clashes with the color of another item, might require accurate pictures that are not easily stored or searched for in currently available conventional databases. While searching for textual information (e.g., skirts in size 7) is easily done, searching for nontext information (e.g., blouses compatible in style with a skirt) is still a problem. Even much text-oriented information that employees need to handle transactions may originate from outside their company and therefore not be readily available in electronic form; thus letters of complaint or explanation that accompany a mail-order return may not be available when the customer next calls up to discuss the status of an order.

Even if the information-intensive tasks that people perform were adequately supported by networked electronic archives, retrieving and processing of information account for only a portion of most people's duties.

Audio and Video Communications

Audio

Speech plays an essential role in our work lives due to its power, expressiveness, and richness in interactive conversation. Numerous studies (e.g., Kraut et al., 1990; Ochsman and Chapanis, 1974) comparing voice and other communications media have repeatedly identified speech as the primary channel for cooperative problem solving. Except in specialized cases, speech plus any medium is better than any other combination of media without speech. Thus, one traditional way for remote workers to keep in touch is to use the telephone. The voice telephone enables real-time communication, supporting interactivity between people that allows them to rapidly get feedback from each other during the course of a conversation. This feedback improves their ability to communicate clearly (Kraut et al., 1982; Clark and Brennan, 1991).

Although the telephone is an old technology (the first call was completed in 1876), several recent developments have contributed to its importance in supporting distributed work. The first is simply the reduction in costs and the related change in cultural attitudes that have made long-distance telephone calls a much more frequently used business tool now than in the past. The second trend is the growing availability of mobile communications that make it much easier to contact workers while they are traveling. Historically, drawbacks to the radio services used by police dispatchers and others who communicate with mobile workers have been their limited geographic range, their high cost, and their very limited availability. In traditional telephony a constraint has been the fact that a telephone number represented a fixed location, not a person. Thus one person attempting to contact another placed calls to the locations where the recipient was most likely to be, and hoped for the best.

Recently, however, both switched and store-and-forward services for mobile workers have become available nationwide. National switched services include paging and the mobile telephone, which signals its presence to local relay cells so that any calls to that mobile telephone number can be routed to the cell then in contact with the mobile telephone. Store-and-forward services include electronic mail and voice mail, which allow a sender to leave in a repository a message that can subsequently be picked up and attended to by the recipient over local or wide area data networks, including the nationwide telecommunications network.

A third trend in telecommunications that enhances telephony's support for distributed work is the introduction of what had been business services or equipment, repackaged for the residential market by communications companies and equipment manufacturers. For example, telephone companies now offer call waiting, call forwarding, three-way calling, calling number identification, and voice mail for the residential market. Relatively inexpensive telecommunications hardware for the home both supplements and competes with the services now embedded in the communications network. Multiline telephones, answering machines, and fax machines are now easily affordable. Both optional communications services and stand-alone devices are disproportionately purchased by people who work from their homes (Dudley et al., 1993).

Video and Audio-Video

Video telephony is another communications development that has implications for distributed work. Video telephones were first demonstrated in 1927 (Ives, 1930). Since then, the telecommunications industry has attempted to solve the technical problems that prevented video telephony from enjoying widespread use. Recent improvements in algorithms for video compression and powerful new microprocessing chips will increase quality and reduce the cost of videophones and conferencing equipment to levels that small businesses and consumers can afford. These developments, along with industry agreement on standards for the interoperability of compression and decompression devices for digital video (codec devices) and the availability of communications services at data rates that support reasonable-quality video transmission, promise to make video tele-phony and videoconferencing more widely used services in the fu-ture.

It seems reasonable to think that a video connection should be especially good at enabling distributed groups to work as if they were in a face-to-face meeting. Yet a substantial body of research literature suggests that the visual medium does little to improve con-versation when the main goal is the exchange of information. How-ever, video connections do seem to have greater value for handling complex, ambiguous, or conflictual tasks and for tasks in which the social component is important (see Williams, 1977, for an early re-view and Fish et al., 1992, and Tang and Isaacs, 1992, for more recent discussions). Compared to audio-only conversations, audio-video conversations are more personalized, less argumentative, and broader in focus. Groups engaging in audio-video conversations tend to like each other more and are more likely to reach consensus easily; in negotiation or persuasion sessions, the negotiation is gentler and agree-ments tend to be influenced by the personalities of the bargainers, rather than resting exclusively on the merits of the argument (Wil-liams, 1977).

In addition, in field trials, new applications of video connections have emerged that go beyond conventional interpersonal communi-cation, including the use of videophones to access multimedia infor-mation services and to maintain organizational awareness. The use of videoconferencing for accessing broadcast materials is common in both business and education settings (LaRose, 1983, cited in Svenning and Ruchinskas, 1984). Users of experimental video telephony sys-tems can place calls to television channels to see the news and other entertainment, and to video cassette recorders to access stored infor-mation. By placing calls to corporate lectures and presentations and thus attending these events remotely, users reduce their risk of wast-ing time, since they can politely turn off an unproductive session or attend to the broadcast and their desk work simultaneously. People have also used video for benign surveillance—to maintain awareness of what their colleagues are doing even when they are not immedi-ately communicating with them. In video telephony field experi-ments, users have maintained long-lived calls to "public" places—lobbies or lunch rooms, for example—just to know what was going on at remote sites. In addition, they have maintained long-lived calls to work partners—for example, people with whom they were co-authoring a document—in order to have easy access to them, but without engaging in sustained conversation. In effect, when they anticipated frequent but unscheduled conversations, they used video to create a shared office for a time. These novel uses were enabled by video; they rarely happen on the voice telephone.

Computer-mediated Communications

Typically, in conventional organizations members acquire much of their technical knowledge and a substantial amount of incidental information by bumping into interesting people or situations (Allen, 1977; Kusterer, 1978; Lave and Wenger, 1991). Members who are at the periphery of an organization have fewer opportunities to converse spontaneously with colleagues and to observe others working or in interaction with each other. Isolated members can thus be at a disadvantage in knowing about their work environment (e.g., Hesses et al., 1993).

Current Uses of Electronic Mail

Electronic mail seems to be an especially useful medium for supporting distributed work because it is able to overcome many disadvantages of working at a distance, especially for isolated members of an organization. Like other asynchronous media, such as facsimile and voice mail, electronic mail allows people to leave messages that are available almost instantaneously regardless of distance but that do not require the sender and recipient of the message to be simultaneously available. In addition, communications sent by electronic mail tend to be processed and archived more easily than communication exchanged using more ephemeral media (e.g., face-to-meetings and telephone calls) or media that are harder to search (e.g., voice mail). Electronic mail as a written document supports a form of memory for distributed work groups, allowing personnel to keep up with communications that have gone on in their absence. Third, because of the ease of sending messages to multiple recipients through on-line bulletin boards and distribution lists, communications sent by electronic mail tend to have more recipients than communication through other media (Kraut and Attewell, 1993; Finholt, 1994), thus facilitating the spread of organizational information.

Several studies have shown that individuals working at an organization's periphery use electronic mail more than those at the core of the organization (Kraut and Attewell, 1993; Finholt, 1994). Compared to those who do not use electronic mail, members of distributed groups who use it regularly tend to know each other better and to be more uniformly involved in the group's projects (Eveland and Bikson, 1988). When isolated members use electronic mail more, they tend to be more informed about their organizations (Kraut and Attewell, 1993; Finholt, 1994) and tend to be more successful. For example, Hesses et al. (1993) have shown that oceanographers who used an electronic mail network for project communication published more articles and had greater professional recognition than did non-users and that the benefits of network use accrued most to the scientists who were geographically isolated (i.e., away from the coasts) or who were less senior.

Potential Uses of Electronic Mail for Distributed Work

Communications technologies are more valuable the more ubiquitous they are. Much of electronic mail's potential for distributed work has not yet been realized, because its use is still significantly concentrated within high-technology organizations and the academic community. The use of electronic mail by unaffiliated individuals and small businesses, and the ability to communicate with people who are not on large networks, is still limited. However, it is growing with the expansion of commercial network providers.

What truly distinguishes electronic mail from other communications media is that electronic mail messages are computational objects. That is, messages are sent and received in a form that can be directly processed by computer. In theory, it is possible to use information retrieval techniques to search through an organization's archives of electronic mail, or use filtering mechanisms to allow intelligent agents to separate important messages from the routine or irrelevant. In practice, however, most commercial electronic mail software packages have only rudimentary searching and filtering capabilities.

It is also possible to anticipate forms of computer-augmented communication that will improve traditional human-to-human communication, rather than merely allowing it to take place at a distance. For example, with some addition of database capabilities, products like Lotus Notes use electronic mail to form the basis for work flow processing. Once designed, certain types of messages can automatically route themselves through the various steps in an organizational process, collecting comments and approvals along the way. This type of application can also be used to consolidate and record organizational knowledge and may be particularly important for distributed organizations and work teams.

Currently, however, few people apply computation to electronic messages, even when these capabilities are available (see Lai et al.,

1988; Flores et al., 1988; and Borenstein, 1992, for examples of systems for computer-augmented human communication). Despite the recent development of "intelligent" electronic mail systems with some searching, filtering, and work-flow-processing capabilities, most electronic mail is apparently still read directly by humans, without the aid of these information-handling tools (Bullen and Bennett, 1991). Additional multidisciplinary research in this general area might improve the ability of software to mimic the filtering, sorting, and processing functions of individuals who have learned to use electronic mail as a central part of their work.

Information Sharing and Use of Remote Facilities

Although the capability to enable remote sharing of expensive instrumentation and facilities has been limited to date, its potential benefits are considerable. Some of the possibilities for using computing and communications technology to facilitate remote field work in oceanography, control of remote instruments in space physics, or real-time sharing of research results in molecular biology have been suggested in *National Collaboratories* (CSTB, 1993). Other distributed and mobile workers will also find it advantageous to be able to control physical devices remotely. For example, the University of California at San Diego recently made an electron microscope available to scientists over the Internet. Users can control many of the functions of the microscope while receiving high-quality images in real time. Applications of this nature need not, however, be limited to the scientific research realm; specialized industrial or medical imaging and testing equipment might also be controlled, and the output viewed, remotely. In general, the value of this capability is highest when either the physical assets or the individuals with the needed knowledge are in short supply, or when the equipment must be operated in a hazardous environment.

Remote control and utilization of data require reliable networking with sufficient bandwidth to support interactive responses between the equipment being controlled and the user receiving the images or other data stream. Expansion of this type of application will require changes to the devices to be controlled, sophisticated distributed control software systems, and creative user interfaces. A particularly challenging application might be to develop a remote control application that would allow scientists to control experimental devices over a wireless personal communication system device or over cellular networks.

THE REALITY OF
TODAY'S DISTRIBUTED WORK

Although distributed work includes telecommuting, it also encompasses activities such as working while mobile, field work, and computer- and telecommunications-assisted education and collaboration. What could once be done only in an office or lecture hall, for example, can now often be accomplished from other sites. Mobility has significant advantages, such as increased temporal and locational flexibility in working and learning, but also disadvantages, for instance, that the time and effort spent to utilize technological capabilities may sometimes seem to outweigh the benefits. At times, what can be envisioned as a productive approach to doing work well is not supported by currently available communications technology and infrastructure.

The Mobile Worker—A Composite

The work experience of "Richard," a prototypical modern mobile executive in a large, multinational organization, simultaneously illustrates the capabilities that today's technology enables and underscores many of the limitations that people undertaking distributed work or telecommuting must face today.

What Richard does can be divided loosely into two categories: (1) "manifest" work activities, performed primarily alone, such as information retrieval and perusal, reading, editing, and document preparation; and (2) communication and related activities involving other individuals. As with many managers and executives, at least half of Richard's time is devoted to communications. There is, of course, an enormous overlap between the two categories, and both tend to be interrupted frequently by external demands.

Richard works in a number of locations, including his office, additional company sites, his home, customer sites, his car, hotel rooms, airplanes, and airports. To support his work and communication needs, Richard relies on an office computer, a home computer, a portable computer, modems, printers, facsimile machines, electronic mail, telephones, and voice mail, and from time to time he accesses his office computer from computers in other offices. On a few occasions, while negotiating a complex deal, he has used a pager.

Because his job is so communication-intensive, much of Richard's computer use is for sending and receiving electronic mail. He estimates that less than 20 percent of his computer use is for his manifest work activities. To accomplish those tasks, he relies heavily on paper because of its portability and ease of manipulation; paper can be carried from place to place, skimmed, studied, and/or marked up with ease.

Given Richard's activity mix, work locations, and the devices on which he relies, what are the main problems he encounters in accomplishing his work?

The main problem Richard is constantly encountering is the lack of integration between his computers and the other devices he uses, and even among the software programs used on his computers. The output from one tool or device can not always be easily input to another. For example, Richard uses four separate electronic mail systems to obtain global coverage but cannot combine them to receive mail in one place. He has a similar problem with his calendar and appointment information, which cannot be easily transferred among systems or made easily accessible to others who are at remote sites. In the office he still must print complex pages or pages containing graphics and physically carry them to the facsimile machine for transmission. This lack of integration inconveniences and irritates Richard and slows his work.

Richard also encounters difficulties related to the complexity of installing, gaining access to, and using tools and devices. He tends to use a small subset of the functionality available in software packages and in complex devices such as facsimile machines. Richard is not fond of interface changes and unexpected incompatibility among systems, and so he often chooses not to upgrade software until his system administrator insists. The other problems he encounters range from relatively minor but annoying circumstances—such as the difficulty of locating electronic mail addresses, the occasional unreliability of electronic mail delivery, and uncertainty about the extent to which a note by electronic mail should be polished and formal like a letter, rather than informal like a voice mail message—to broader, less defined concerns about issues like privacy and security.

Richard's use of a laptop computer illustrates many of the above problems and some additional issues as well. He has yet to discover a simple, foolproof method of keeping the programs, information, and files on his laptop synchronized with those on his office and home computers. Technical support is an even greater problem for the laptop than for his home computer: the portable computer is generally used both away from the office and during off hours when the office is closed. Even worse, he often does not know what electronic files he will need when he goes to a meeting away from his home office, and he would prefer to be able to connect to his office and access electronic information from the meeting site with equipment located there. He thinks that, ideally, he should be able to access his electronic mail and files, exchange electronic information with others physically present at the meeting, and set up a remote information world without having had to carry anything at all to the meeting. In short, he wishes that the computing environment at his various meeting sites would enable him to obtain all the computer-based information support he could get at his office if he were physically present there.

Richard still feels that the laptop is too obtrusive for taking notes during really important meetings. He has considered getting a personal digital assistant just for use in such circumstances, but he doesn't want yet another device to carry and he has heard that the handwriting recognition is poor. Richard therefore typically relies on pencil-and-paper notes and tries to type up the important ones to save on the portable computer for easy referral. He is intrigued by the use of computers during meetings for tasks such as brainstorming but is concerned that he will not be able to communicate his ideas as effectively as he does when speaking. Richard has used his computer a few times to prepare presentations. He found that it required a great deal of time to get everything colored, spaced, and sized properly for visual appeal, in contrast to the times when he used the company's graphics department.

Modem use is essential during Richard's time away from his office. However he rarely finds that he can just plug the modem in and use it, especially when he is traveling internationally. He often cannot access his electronic mail when he wants to, or feels that he wastes time in getting connected. His success in sending facsimiles from hotel rooms using his own portable computer is even lower. And at the moment, his portable computer cannot receive and display facsimiles.

Richard's problems with printers are "simple." His home printer does not have the quality, speed, or reliability he would like. A printer is rarely available when he is traveling and when one is available, he often has trouble connecting to it and getting his software to print documents properly. On some occasions, he has resorted to sending himself a fax, in essence using a facsimile machine as a printer.

People sometimes joke that Richard has a telephone attached to the side of his head. He still relies heavily on the telephone and voice mail for communication. He identifies fewer difficulties with telephone use than computer use. The problems he encounters are the quantity of numbers he needs to remember and the expense and occasionally the poor quality of cellular telephone use. Because Richard frequently works from home and sometimes while on vacation, he wants to be accessible without letting people know where he is. Instead, he finds all too often that he leaves three or four telephone numbers with someone when he wants to be reachable. He has occasionally used a pager when he wanted to ensure that he could be reached immediately.

Richard has found that voice mail is a necessary addition to telephone communications. He likes the informality and personal nature of voice mail but sometimes must rerecord a message to convey the desired tone. He wishes he could be notified more easily of waiting messages, especially important ones. He also wishes he could skim, prioritize, filter, and save the text of messages, just as he can with electronic mail. Yet the convenience and availability of telephone use, compared to computer use, mean that Richard uses voice mail much more heavily than electronic mail. He is occasionally concerned about the privacy of voice mail, especially given the ease of forwarding it within his system. But at the same time, he wishes that his company would integrate all its voice mail systems so that he could forward messages to anyone in the company.

Expense also is an issue, especially to the management in Richard's company. He would like to explore some new technologies, such as ways of connecting his various communication devices or the use of videoconferencing to reduce his travel and allow impromptu meetings, but he is unable to justify the cost. He is nervous about increasing the number of technological devices he needs to know how to operate or use, even though he imagines that it would be great to call a meeting quickly and use videoconferencing to have it, rather than having to plan it far enough in advance that everyone can schedule it and travel to a common site for it. Richard is concerned that skills that he has refined over his career will become less effective with the introduction of other ways of accomplishing work; in particular, his ability to dominate conversations is well refined and has contributed to his success. He also wonders about his ability to manage his work time and personal family time. It sometimes seems that his manager now has unlimited expectations regarding Richard's availability since there are now fewer technical boundaries no matter what the hour of the day is or where he is located—even when he is on vacation. Although the discomfort that many managers feel at supervising people who are connected but not often visible has been cited as a significant problem with mobile work, major problems also exist for the mobile worker regarding the management of work and family boundaries.

There are thus several general problems Richard encounters in his use of multiple devices and communication channels. One is that the amount of technical expertise needed for effective use far exceeds his desired level of knowledge. Much of what he does is too time-consuming, and the lack of integration and interoperability is a constant source of frustration. Solutions may exist to some of Richard's problems, but he is not aware of them or he is hesitant to implement the significant changes to his work habits that would be required. He also feels that he now must do himself much of the work that used to be done by his assistant. With important communications being transmitted via so many different media, he particularly misses the ability his assistant used to have to filter and prioritize calls, messages, and written information.

In summary, Richard wants significantly better integration of devices, services, and interfaces regardless of whether he is in his office or mobile. He needs better ways to manage and integrate the ever increasing flows of information arriving on multiple media from multiple sources. In the long term, he wants a ubiquitous computing environment such as that being explored at Xerox PARC (Weiser, 1993) so that he can largely dispense with "hoofing around" so much technology and so many information sources himself.

Distributed Education

Much like mobile work, education currently makes use of several technologies to achieve some locational independence, and could use even better tools to increase educational effectiveness. The United States, Great Britain, and many European countries have a long tradition of offering distance learning using paper, television, and more recently, computer-augmented instruction. Commercial and public television has been used to broadcast college-level courses for decades, and corporate teleconferencing and closed-circuit networks have been used for broadcasting training materials since their earliest days (see, e.g., LaRose, 1983). The National Technological University broadcasts more than 25,000 hours of educational material and short courses to more than 130 corporate clients per year (NTU, 1994). In a typical distance education application, a lecture is specially organized for noninteractive, video delivery and is broadcast to subscribers, who view it as it is transmitted or record it for later playback. These broadcast lectures are often supplemented with a telephone connection, so that members of a remote audience can ask questions or make comments to the lecturer. In a variant of this model, Stanford University's School of Engineering (Gibbons et al., 1977) has videotaped regular college lecture courses and then shown them unedited to students from industry in off-campus locations. The tapes are shipped to remote sites with homework assignments and examinations. An on-site tutor guides the students through the lecture, encouraging them to stop frequently for questions and discussion. In the 1980s and 1990s, electronic mail and bulletin boards and other tools have been added to the more traditional video media to support interaction among students and between students and instructors (Hiltz, 1993).

The use of technology to support distance education has obvious benefits. It allows experts to be more productive by distributing their expertise to a wider audience. It supports students who are physically removed from schools and universities or who are isolated from a critical mass of other students who share their educational needs. Using asynchronous technology like videotapes also allows students to study at times convenient to them. Similarly, they can stop and start the instruction at will, which can be an advantage in trying to understand material that is especially difficult or that is presented in a language other than a student's own native language.

Despite these advantages, the current technology to support distance learning places substantial constraints on the educational enterprise. It is no surprise that current distance learning applications typically use a lecture style of instruction, since the technology is conducive to this model of information transmission. Whether live or on video, today's lecture setting is characterized by the isolation of the instructor, a low degree of social interaction, a low level of attention to individual students, and a declarative model of learning. For example, while at a lecture, students generally cannot make use of archived information, and interaction typically is limited to a few questions and answers. The pace of information delivery is not under the student's control; it must be modulated by the teacher in response to his or her assessment of average student readiness or understanding. While the content of most educational material is declarative, the goal of much educational instruction is to impart procedural knowledge, the basis for doing rather than describing.

Educators and others can imagine the value of remote instruction that incorporates features of the workplace, thereby enabling substantial interaction among students, access to personal archives, and hands-on experience with work objects like models, experiments, or instruments—for example, a remotely taught collaborative design course in which industrial design students work with human-factors specialists and software engineers to build a wearable computer (Smailagic and Siewiorek, 1994). Unfortunately, the capability for remote participants in distance learning to have highly interactive discussions to plan and develop a design is not supported well by current communications technologies or applications. Neither audio- nor videoconferences deal well with multiple voice channels, or with the starts, stops, and interruptions that characterize animated group discussions (see, e.g., O'Conaill et al., 1992) Similarly, while electronic mail and computerized bulletin boards are good for involving many participants and for keeping records of a conversation, they do not handle well the give-and-take discussions that many groups need to have when clarifying ideas.

Some experiments using more interactive technology such as two-way video for distance learning are now under way (e.g., National Geographic's Kid's Net for geography and ocean sciences education). These experiments emphasize collaborative learning and in the process are developing tools for distributed work that are specialized for educational settings, especially for the K-12 age groups. However, techniques for operating equipment and instruments at a distance, for receiving output, and for sharing output among multiple students are in their infancy.

Collaborative Work—The Need for New Products Linked to Underlying Databases or Objects

One of the reasons for the success of electronic mail is its similarity to current work practices: it resembles other forms of message sending and information circulation. However, many of the most successful collaborative projects are based on a model that has a closer technological match in physical objects or database technology. For example, when people work together they often co-locate and share writing, drawings, physical space, and mental space. They communicate through gesturing at a shared image or section of text. They suggest changes that can easily be seen, evaluated, and further changed by colleagues (Whitaker and Geelhoed, 1993; Fish et al., 1992). Unfortunately, most group and distributed work products still depend on easy-to-accept electronic mail-based models of work augmented by some shared-screen capabilities. Products, like Lotus Notes, based on underlying databases are now only beginning to be developed and marketed.

Facsimile transmission allows remote workers to quickly transmit and share static documents but not to jointly manipulate them during the course of a conversation. Several software packages and technology being developed for audio- and videoconferencing over the Internet allow people whose computers are on a common data network to jointly view and manipulate computer files and computer screens. Unfortunately, unlike telephones or fax machines, which have a level of standardization such that virtually any fax or tele-phone in the world can communicate with any other, these file- and screen-sharing programs are not standardized and do not interoperate. Therefore these applications work only with careful planning and agreement among people who use compatible combinations of hard-ware and software.

Although current products have facilitated writing and composi-tion for many individuals, much collaborative writing and revision continue to be done primarily by people who are either temporarily or permanently co-located. The still painful nature of collaborating in such tasks via electronic mail is evidenced by the various editing "protocols" that have evolved from the use of current word proces-sors and electronic mail to coauthor or revise a document: to circum-vent the main goal of the design of word processors—making changes visible as soon as possible and always keeping what is displayed on the screen as close as possible in form and appearance to the final output—authors collaborating via electronic mail often must differ-entiate new text from old text, or comments on existing text, by changing the appearance of the new text or marking existing text with a ">" mark at the beginning of each line. By using these somewhat con-trived conventions, they can better communicate changes and dis-cuss them before agreeing on a final version.

Emerging products such as PREP, developed at Carnegie Mellon University, and Shredit, developed at the University of Michigan, hold promise for facilitating writing and editing by geographically distributed groups. What distributed authors need—and what the market is only slowly starting to provide—is reengineered programs that can leverage database technology to support collaborative build-ing of documents, diagrams, presentations, and other application ob-jects. In other words, the conventional word processor, designed for individual use and highly evolved for layout and production of pa-per documents, needs to be rethought and recast as a group writing tool. It must have all the power of a great word processor, but it must also be built with distributed database technology to support work at a distance in which the document is shared in an environ-ment of heterogeneous hardware, software, and network systems.

THE POTENTIAL FOR INCREASED DISTRIBUTED WORK

Distributed work, including telecommuting, is almost certain to increase in the next decade. Even using a comparatively narrow definition of telecommuting, the U.S. Department of Transportation

(1993) has estimated, for example, that, the current number of telecommuters is about 2.0 million and will grow to between 7.5 million and 15 million by the year 2002. Although the exact extent of the increase is difficult to predict, the following factors will be important contributors to an expanded potential for distributed work:

• *If you wire it, they will come*—As long as the National Information Infrastructure includes two-way connections, the expected growth in telecommunications capacity for the home and for potential satellite office sites will make the services needed for effective telecommuting and distributed work more widely available and probably less expensive on a unit basis. As higher-bandwidth networks and high-capacity telecommunication links become more widely available, for example, opportunities will increase for the appropriate use of high-quality audio and video links to enable the work of distributed project teams.

• *The real estate imperative*—Corporate America is starting to realize that the term "fixed overhead" need not apply to office space. As staff sizes are reduced, employees are relocated to customer sites, and some employees choose to engage in distributed work for their own reasons, an increasing number of companies will consider reducing costs by reducing the size of their facilities, including high-overhead meeting rooms.

• *Moving beyond working at home to remote work*—The United States is catching up to worldwide interest in satellite offices, rural telework centers, and other hybrid work sites intermediate between the home and the central office. To the extent that these options overcome real or perceived problems of telecommuting from the home, and to the extent that they offer job-creation possibilities, they will become more prevalent. This development will shift the focus of both distributed workers and policymakers away from a model involving 10 people, each working at home 20 miles from the office 2 days a week, to one of 100 people working in a rural telecenter 500 miles from the office 5 days a week. The scope, the stakes, and the potential economic benefits are much larger.

• *Life beyond bureaucracy*—Whether the eventual result is a virtual corporation, a series of strategic alliances, or massive "outsourcing," we are moving into an era in which the traditional, full-employment corporation that does its own work with its own employees may become the exception instead of the rule. Removing the boundaries of the traditional organizational chart is likely to alter the assumption that centralization of the work force is inherently a good idea.

It may be that the most agile and competitive organizations in the next few decades will be those with the best networks—networks in the broad sense of interconnected people, telecommunications, information resources, suppliers, production capabilities, and customers. Distributed work tools that facilitate collaboration, reduce travel, and track complex projects across several organizations will be in great demand to support such an organizational structure. The nation will benefit through improved competitiveness, and individuals will benefit as locational barriers to employment are reduced. However, researchers and policymakers will need to pay considerable attention to integrating the new work styles and technologies in a way that yields optimal social and economic benefits while minimizing market disruptions.

3

Distributed Work and Group Processes

Distributed work has implications for many of the activities that organizations, groups, and individuals need to accomplish to be effective; its wider adoption will present both organizational and personal challenges. Technology is likely to solve only a subset of these challenges, but nonetheless should be developed and applied when appropriate.

The impact of distributed work on group processes and performance is worthy of examination because group performance encompasses individual performance, because so much of the work in organizations is done by groups, and because organizations themselves have functions that parallel those of groups (Katz and Kahn, 1979). Reviewing the voluminous research literature on groups and organizations is beyond the scope of this report. Rather, the intent in this chapter is to point out group processes most likely to be affected by the distribution of work across space and time and to discuss basic functions that must be supported for distributed work to be conducted effectively.

Such functions go beyond tasks with a single focus such as writing a report, selling a product, or handling a customer's transaction. Individuals in organizations are typically members of multiple groups, each of which is involved in multiple projects. As members of groups, people perform their assigned work tasks, as well as many ancillary activities that keep them coordinated, motivated, well trained, and adapted to their organizational context. Moreover, individuals may well play different roles in different groups: leader in some, member in others; expert in some, novice in others; and so on.

DISTRIBUTED WORK IN THE CONTEXT OF BUSINESS ORGANIZATIONS

Even though businesses are not identically structured, they share similarities that can be discussed usefully in terms of the effects of distributed work. Every organization has two primary, albeit competing, needs: to divide labor into the various tasks that need to be performed and to coordinate these tasks so that the overall goals of the organization can be met. As management theorist Henry Mintzberg (1979) has written, the "structure of an organization can be defined simply as the sum total of the ways in which it divides its labor into distinct tasks and then achieves coordination among them." According to Mintzberg, each relatively large business organization consists of three basic parts: (1) an operating core that has as its primary function the fundamental work of producing goods and/or services; (2) an administrative component that provides strategic management, middle or line management, and technical services and leadership; and (3) a support staff that provides ancillary services such as legal counsel and personnel, finance, communications, and building services.

Any introduction of technology into an organization must take into account both the nature of the technology and where in the organization the technology is introduced. Introducing advanced robotics on the shop floor will yield a very different relationship between technology and organizational culture than will increasing the availability of laptop computers, cellular telephones, and modems in the ranks of middle management or at the strategic apex of the corporation. The introduction of new technologies to facilitate distributed work is simply a particular case of the broad interaction between organizations and technology.

While distributed work in almost all cases means increased independence of place for the worker, how it plays out precisely will vary according to the kind of work, the intention of the worker, and the area within the organization in which it occurs. In some cases, "knowledge" workers can work outside of the centralized office—at home or in a satellite office—so as to achieve greater mental concentration or a more desirable lifestyle. Much of the contemporary discussion regarding telecommuting concerns this aspect of distributed work. In other cases, distributed work may mean that employees will travel less to the centralized office—because they now have access to information or services that once would have required them to make trips into the office—and travel more freely and frequently to clients or to other operating plants.

For example, advanced technology currently allows more time in the field for General Electric Company service staff. A GE service technician returns home at the end of each day and uses a laptop computer and modem to obtain assignments for the next day, order parts necessary to replenish inventory, and order whatever special equipment may be needed for the next day's calls. While the technician sleeps, the van, still sitting in his or her driveway, is restocked, saving a trip to a parts depot and allowing for more repair time the following day. Such a work arrangement requires fundamental changes in core work concepts and practices: inventory is delivered to technicians rather than having to be picked up at parts depots, and assignments are obtained at home rather than at the office. The technician's data become part of a larger performance management system so that management can track trends in the nature of service calls, anticipate preventive maintenance needs, and so on.

Distributed work can enhance productivity and locational independence for a variety of work purposes. The various approaches chosen by individuals and organizations to fulfill their particular purposes are almost certain to gain increased attention and importance over the coming years. Distributed work also raises questions regarding the impacts of various work arrangements on the individual and on the culture and functioning of organizations. In addition to the technological research outlined in this report, extensive sociological and organizational research will be required to ensure that distributed work can be carried out to serve the needs of individuals and organizations effectively.

STRATEGIES FOR ACCOMMODATING
DISTRIBUTED WORK

According to estimates by the U.S. Department of Transportation (1993), more than 2 million people currently telecommute in the United States, and more than 10 times as many work at home under other arrangements, including corporate after-hours work or various forms of self-employment. In addition, large numbers of people travel as a routine part of their jobs: sales people travel to customer sites, maintenance personnel travel to immobile equipment, and executives travel to meetings, for example. Yet currently available technology for distributed work places substantial constraints on the types of work and learning that can be done remotely from a central site, on the road, or removed from peers and supervisors.

When a work group is co-located and physically embedded within a larger organization, many of the processes necessary for success are tacit or informal. People learn the norms of an organization and many job-relevant behaviors by observing the people around them. Supervisors manage groups by monitoring employee effort, recognizing and averting incipient failure, helping resolve personality conflicts, appraising performance, and providing advice and instruction. Workers may call over to a colleague at the next desk for help. They share budgets, designs, or machinery by simply gathering in a common physical place with the appropriate facilities, such as a white board or overhead projector, or with the item under discussion. Substantial research suggests, however, that while these informal and tacit processes are common, they are not invariably the best ones for ensuring organizational effectiveness. Workers may, for example, learn norms of minimal work effort by being able to ask a convenient local for advice while ignoring an expert farther away. And, as organizations become larger and more specialized, these informal processes often become increasingly impractical.

When members of a work group are physically separated from each other or from a supporting organizational structure, tacit and informal processes no longer suffice to support group work and organizational effectiveness. Groups need different strategies for handling group formations, operations, external relations, and reorganization. The approaches that can be taken are of three major types.

- Organizations can attempt to reduce the interdependence among distributed group members. Studies of telecommuting and home-based employment suggest that reducing interdependence is a common mode of coping with a distributed work force in the face of inadequate communications facilities. For example, companies occasionally reduce the interdependence between supervisor and employee by paying piece rates or by creating independent contractor arrangements. Consultants may tend to recommend only stand-alone jobs such as writing manuals as being suitable for telecommuting. Scientists working remotely from each other may engage in a more formal division of labor and may communicate less among themselves.

- Firms can attempt to reproduce at a distance the informality of the processes typically supported by physical proximity and, in so doing, may reproduce both the adequacies and the inadequacies of the informal processes. For example, some organizations have deployed electronic mail and computer conferencing to support informal communication, discussion, and decision making. In several organizational experiments, long-duration video connections between remote work sites have also been used to support informal communication (Abel et al., 1990; Fish et al., 1992; Bly et al., 1993).

• Alternatively, organizations can attempt to use managerial and technological mechanisms to formalize at a distance the processes normally supported by proximity-based informal communication. For example, tools currently exist to facilitate the successful development of software programs by geographically distributed teams. Typically, a highly specialized database is used to track the programmers' progress and coordinate the program segments that have been placed within a globally distributed file system.

BASIC GROUP PROCESSES
TO BE SUPPORTED FOR
EFFECTIVE DISTRIBUTED WORK

Despite the use of strategies for handling decentralized work, several group and organizational processes are likely to be disrupted by the distribution of work over space and time. Among these are the selection of goals, recruitment of group members, management of distributed groups, and information retrieval. Sketched below for each is the way the process is generally performed in a centralized organization, how distributed work might disrupt the process, technological solutions that might mitigate such disruption, and, if applicable, application and infrastructure research needed to implement these solutions.

Selecting Goals

The process of selecting initial goals depends on the type of group being formed. For some groups, such as a crisis task force, the group goal is largely predefined. However, in other groups, like senior management teams, quality improvement circles, or teams of collaborating scientists, specific goals often emerge from informal communication. This communication can occur in distributed communication environments through the use of electronic bulletin boards or electronic mail distribution lists, or through the use of real-time audio- or videoconferences. The technical challenge is to support both casual and formal small-group communication to facilitate the formulation, evaluation, and selection of goals in distributed work groups. Today, the traditional written medium is generally too slow for the give and take through which new, shared ideas emerge and goals are

selected. Computer-facilitated communication is faster but often re-
duces social context cues, thereby blurring the link between what is
being said and the person saying it and thus reducing the likelihood
that consensual goals will emerge.

Recruiting Group Members

In addition to determining an initial project goal, the most important processes in forming a project group are identifying, investigat-
ing, and recruiting potential members.

Substantial research literature suggests that physical proximity
plays a large role in forming teams. As Hagstrom (1965) noted over
25 years ago, "since collaboration often begins through informal contacts, anything that increases the frequency of such contacts increases
the likelihood of collaboration. . . . Spatial propinquity often leads to
collaboration since it is likely to lead to informal communication."
Of course, more recent experiences with electronic networks suggest
new options for stimulating informal communication, although it may
be too early to tell how productive they are.

During the initiation phase of a collaboration, potential collaborators must establish an intellectual and interpersonal relationship
based on shared interests. Selecting people and ideas are both important and often intertwined. Physical proximity creates opportunities for potential collaborators to become acquainted, to assess and
develop interpersonal compatibility, to identify common interests, to
explore new ideas, and to accomplish rudimentary planning before
they become committed to working together. In this way, individuals determine whether potential partners are smart enough to help
think through problems, responsible enough to do their share of the
work, and humble enough to accept only their share of the credit, as
well as whether they are sympathetic enough with one's perspective
and compatible enough in work style and personality to make working together pleasant. Sometimes collaborations come about simply
because the potential collaborators like each other, before they have
any shared ideas to work on.

While research collaborations and other types of ad hoc groups
can and do form at a distance, the evidence indicates they are much
less likely to do so than if the potential members are or have been co-
located. Nevertheless, despite the barriers, some amount of scientific
research has always been carried out by individuals who share common or complementary interests but happen to be located at different
institutions. Notably, scientists have been among the early adopters

of network, data communication, and computing technologies, the most basic tools and technologies needed for collaboration at a distance. In addition, supervision is generally less of an issue in scientific research teams than in project teams in other areas.

Although members of a team are often identified and evaluated informally, database and information retrieval technology could aid in the selection process for distributed workers on at least some dimensions. For example, it is theoretically possible to apply the statistical techniques used in information retrieval to a database of research personnel. Potential candidates for a work group could be represented by the documents they have written or textual descriptions of the projects they have worked on. Queries against such a database could return information on the relevance of each candidate to the query, subject of course to the known inaccuracies of information retrieval systems. In the case of seeking a partner for scientific collaboration, a query of the published literature could return a list of researchers who have, for example, applied factor analysis to the problem of second language learning.

Such techniques, however, do not currently suffice for identifying people with the personal attributes and skills necessary for a particular work group. The insufficiency is not intrinsic to an information retrieval approach to personnel recruiting, but occurs because personal attributes are seldom articulated explicitly by people seeking to form groups and, more importantly, because this information is now rarely recorded in organizational archives about projects or people. For example, effective group work may require individuals with a sense of humor, creative or leadership abilities, and a willingness to do their share of the work; knowledge of such attributes as they apply to individuals is most often uncovered through informal conversations with people who have worked with these individuals before. Of course, this phenomenon is also reflected in conventional hiring procedures, in which substantial screening is done based on resumes or comparable documentation but final decisions tend to be based on interviews and consultations with references.

The ability to assess personal, work-relevant attributes from databases of public-record materials or, more likely, to interact informally with individuals who could attest to such attributes could promote more effective, efficient formation of distributed work groups (assuming that privacy, liability, and other ancillary social and legal considerations can be accommodated). Social scientists and computer scientists should consider joint research aimed at providing a database structure that could aid in the formation of distributed groups.

Managing Distributed Groups

Typically employees in groups distributed at two or three different locations (usually in different time zones and often in different countries) are charged with completing a development task by working collaboratively with their remote colleagues. The development target could be a new piece of hardware, a new financial product, an advertising campaign, and so on. Each site contains several people, at least some of whom have worked together before. And at least some of those people know some of the people at the other sites. Typically the project manager is co-located with the employees at one of the sites.

The first management problem is building one cohesive group out of distributed subgroups. How can technology be used to help people create shared mental models, shared goals, and trust? Technology such as videoconferences may even inadvertently subvert this process by setting up unintended "we/they" dynamics. Project reporting and tracking are more difficult across multiple sites and are exacerbated as project schedules become more complex. The integration of the work products of each site may become an issue if the project involves intellectual or creative efforts that are only marginally suited to detailed specification. Finally, it may be difficult to evaluate the relative contributions of the different groups and individuals on a distributed team.

Obtaining Information

To function successfully within modern organizations, individuals and groups must have increasing amounts of information. Given adequate data transmission links, conventional information systems can currently provide many workers the core information they need. Thus, reservation clerks, directory assistance operators, and even reference librarians working from home can easily obtain needed information from the same information systems they would use in centralized job settings.

Text-based Electronic Sources

Many library collections and other archives of books, articles, and text-oriented documents are becoming increasingly available over general-purpose computer networks such as the Internet. As more of this information becomes available, facilities to browse and search it become increasingly important. More than 30 years of research on information retrieval, coming primarily from a library science perspective, can be applied to the problem of helping people find information when they have a relatively well defined informational need (Salton and McGill, 1979). However, recent experience shows that current query techniques are much less effective for very large databases, or collections of databases, especially if the user is unfamiliar with the underlying detailed structure of the information or database. Often, even the best retrieval systems return only a portion of the material that is relevant to a query, while at the same time returning other material that is irrelevant.

Paper Sources

Currently, much of the information workers receive and would like to have available in multiple locations or to share with others does not arrive in electronic form. While newspaper articles, consultants' reports, and company memos may exist electronically during some stage in their life cycles, they often come to one's desk in paper form. To share hard copy with a colleague electronically is a cumbersome process. A user needs tools to easily convert paper sources of information back into electronic form and to ship, store, and retrieve them. The individual parts for these tools are commercially available in the form of scanners, optical character recognition systems, facsimile machines, multimedia databases, and multimedia electronic mail. However, they are still separate and sizable hardware items, some are still largely outside mainstream use, and users must be familiar with the details of hardware and software compatibility, file formats, image resolution, and other technical details.

Individual Sources

Empirical studies of how managers, scientists, and other knowledge workers search for and use information shows that text-oriented documents are not necessarily the most sought after or the most valuable information in many circumstances. In science, for example, because of their timeliness and relevance to problems at hand, personal contacts and the "gray literature" in a discipline are often as valuable as the published literature (Garvey et al., 1970), which often involves long lead-times for publication. Thus, scientists often know about new findings in their field well before they appear in conference proceedings or archival journals. When attempting to solve a problem, scientists, engineers, and sales personnel are as likely to get help from colleagues as they are to find information in any written source (Constant et al., 1994; Culnan, 1983; Kraut and Streeter, 1994; Tushman, 1977). For example, an individual needing to understand or apply a new statistical technique is as likely to seek guidance from a local expert as from books on statistics or journal articles that have used the technique. (Whether this underuse of the archival literature is desirable or is more a reflection of the poor tools for information search is a question worthy of research in its own right.) In many other circumstances, individuals' personal stores of information are more valuable than new information gleaned from a library. Assuming that the widespread use of individuals' knowledge stores and interpersonal queries is desirable, supporting their use in distributed organizations suggests several directions for research.

Information Sharing

A special problem in supporting distributed work groups and organizations is ensuring that people who have useful information will provide it to others. Within organizations, colleagues and experts often respond to the requests of others for information. The problem with respect to answering such questions is that self-interest can discourage actions that promote the public good. Thus, while many people benefit from having others in an organization contribute their expertise on various topics, it can also be in an individual's interest to take advantage of these databases without contributing to them (Thorn and Connolly, 1987). For example, with properly designed networks and software, a question about using a particular statistical technique might be posed on a university-wide network. Using new indexing mechanisms, the posting could be directed to a small group of campus members with relevant expertise instead of being broadcast to the entire campus or merely posted on a computer bulletin board. These experts could be encouraged to provide answers by systems that implement payment of a royalty for information, that archive particular requests for later use by others, or that highlight an expert's similarity to or identification with the person asking the questions.

In many conventional organizations, information gatekeepers play a special role in spreading needed knowledge (Tushman, 1977; Allen, 1977). These people typically have knowledge of the information needs of other group members, sources of information both within and outside the group, and the communication skills and organizational motivation to proactively connect the two. Research on this type of selective dissemination of information has been ongoing for almost 25 years (Foltz and Dumais, 1993; Gentile and Houseman, 1970), but it has been based on conventional information retrieval techniques. Future research should also consider the dissemination of information in electronic form.

4

Facilitating Distributed Work

IDENTIFYING BARRIERS TO EXPANSION
OF DISTRIBUTED WORK

In addition to the organizational and social processes that constrain adoption of distributed work, there are many technical barriers to its wider acceptance. Good database technology is not in place yet; applications in current use are expressed as massive, monolithic code structures that cannot easily be rewritten; and new applications operate in ways that are not as familiar as the message-passing routines of electronic mail and will therefore meet resistance from customers. Although many of the technical and design issues can be addressed in research laboratories, the issue of user acceptance must be considered at other levels as well: until software producers see a sufficient market for these products, for example, they may be reluctant to make the large investment in research and software development required to overcome the significant barriers.

Complexity-of-Use Barriers

Today, to effectively engage in distributed work or telecommuting, one must absorb a large amount of technical detail and have access to an array of equipment. Before they can become ubiquitous, the systems and equipment must be made easier to understand, and certainly easier to use. For example, a sales person who needs to access a customer accounts database while at home or traveling must have, at a practical minimum, a V.22bis-standard, 2,400-bps modem connected to, or internal to, a portable computer; communications software; and an analog telephone line with an accessible RJ11, or similar, standard jack. Additionally, most communications software packages require that the user be at least minimally aware of communications parameters such as baud rate, parity, data bits, stop bits, and local echo. All of these requirements may be fairly easy to manage at home. However, if a hotel or customer site lacks telephone jacks, or has only digital telephone lines, accessing the customer database can be impossible. In fact, inveterate mobile workers can sometimes be identified by the contents of their well-stocked portable computer cases: screwdrivers and pliers to disassemble telephones, various patch cords with alternate telephone plugs or alligator clips, handset adapters, audio-coupled modems, and digital line adapters. Users who need to have full, mobile access to their company's computer networks must master additional levels of technical sophistication ranging from integrated services digital network (ISDN) telephone line standards to the technicalities of Internet addressing and packet transport protocols.

Inconsistent and inadequate user interfaces also increase complexity-of-use barriers and interfere with the adoption of new computing and communications technology. This is particularly true for distributed workers, who may find themselves using a variety of communications devices and services but in ways only incidental to their primary work tasks or to the primary use of the communications device. For example, it is often a matter of trial and error to determine which of the many services possibly used by a mobile worker, such as call waiting or cellular telephone services, interfere (and in exactly what way) with particular computer communications and how this interference can be eliminated. Often, the ability of end users to take full advantage of flexible and programmable services is limited by cryptic user interfaces based on touch-tone telephone keypads.

Consistency of interfaces and connections across a range of environments are equally important to the mobile worker. Today, for example, a cellular telephone user often needs to make several attempts to dial a long-distance call while roaming in another cellular provider's system. This will certainly become exacerbated when users more routinely wander from areas with high-bandwidth, multimedia connections, to localities with low-bandwidth connections, to remote locations providing high bandwidth from a distant network host. Ubiquity of capabilities—the common denominator, which may be relatively low—will be a key constraint on the speed of distributed work applications.

For the foreseeable future, learning to use networks effectively will require a great deal of human support. It has even been possible to make a business out of providing that support. For example, Omnet, the network company that provides electronic mail and bulletin board services to oceanographers, has a toll-free telephone number enabling an oceanographer to talk to a real person who will tell him/her how to set the parity bits or the local access phone number for accessing electronic mail from Bogota, Bulgaria, or Burlington. Omnet also manages electronic mail distribution lists for distributed projects, ensuring that everyone's electronic mail address is up-to-date and providing hard-copy postal or facsimile delivery to people without electronic mail. Other value-added network vendors offer similar services. More generally, the spread of sophisticated computer-based technologies from the sophisticated pioneering user base into the general population has increased the need for support services, which are provided by both employers and system vendors.

Cost-of-Technology Barriers

The most difficult challenge is how to deploy high-speed communications networks, connections, and equipment at a reasonable price and on a wide scale. As the National Information Infrastructure is advanced and the nation's economy becomes increasingly dependent on information, equitable and inexpensive access will be important to a very large segment of the population. Inclusive policies and deployment decisions will best serve both public and private interests (CSTB, 1994b) and permit wider utilization of distributed work practices. In fact, many modern information technologies depend on wide utilization for their effectiveness and efficiency.

For example, it is instructive to examine the recent, rapid spread of facsimile machines. The basic principles of facsimile transmission were developed in 1842 and thus precede even the telegraph (*McGraw-Hill Encyclopedia of Science & Technology*, 1987). The first significant commercial use was by large news organizations that began sending "wirephotos" in the 1930s. However, the high cost and low speed of the early equipment severely restrained adoption of the technology. Office use began to increase with the introduction of digital facsimile equipment and lower-cost long-distance telephone service in the late 1970s. In the early 1990s inexpensive integrated circuit chips became available, speeds increased, prices dropped drastically, and a "critical mass" of installed machines was reached. The market almost literally exploded, and the least expensive of the machines became home consumer items.

If telecommuting and other forms of distributed work are to increase, lower-cost communication devices and services will be needed. In 1993, high-speed modems generally cost between $100 and $350, and faster ISDN terminal adapters were about twice as expensive, still without offering the bandwidth needed for multimedia and video applications. Video codecs, devices necessary for serious two-way, real-time video work, cost 10 times the amount of current ISDN adapters. Additionally, inexpensive, high-quality displays are clearly needed. Currently a good-quality 17-inch computer monitor, which is generally considered necessary for serious desktop publishing efforts, costs $1,200 or more. This will need to decrease by a factor of at least three before it will be affordable to most users. While general market forces will probably continue to reduce unit prices, researchers and individuals making decisions about distributed work should remember the importance of reducing prices for both infrastructure items and services.

DESIGNING COMMUNICATIONS INFRASTRUCTURE TO SUPPORT A RANGE OF CAPABILITIES FOR DISTRIBUTED WORK

High-speed, broadband communications will be needed to handle the multimedia environment envisioned for both distributed work and the National Information Infrastructure. The next few years should see increasing amounts of bandwidth available due to the deployment of new network facilities and services such as asynchronous transfer mode (ATM) and other broadband network backbones running at speeds ranging from 45 megabits per second to a gigabit per second, or more. However, most of the research in this area has focused on point-to-point communications of a single medium; almost nothing has been done in the area of multiparty, multimedia technologies.

Supporting Typical Work Routines

Currently, the ability to engage in distributed work depends to a large extent on the availability of communications services to support typical activities of an individual or group working remotely, such as the following:

- Contacting another individual, or a group of individuals, using regular telephones and circuits;
- Exchanging messages by electronic mail, voice mail, or facsimile transmission;
- Exchanging documents or images by electronic mail or facsimile transmission;
- Accessing and using computers or computer networks from a remote location, an activity often referred to as a remote log-on;
- Sharing computer files locally and remotely by using explicit schemes such as file transfer protocols, or by using indirect techniques such as distributed file environments; and
- Engaging in videoconferences with participants at two or more locations.

These activities impose different requirements for data transmission rate, or bandwidth, on the supporting technologies. The data transmission rate is a measure of the speed with which a given technology can exchange data and is normally measured in bits per second (bps). The size of data objects (e.g., pages of text, still images, digitized audio clips, movie-like sequences of still images) is measured in bits, and dividing the size of the data object by the transmission rate yields the minimum time that it takes for an object to be transmitted, disregarding any "overhead" for processes like error checking and retransmission. In practice, about 10 percent of the bandwidth is lost to overhead in asynchronous communications. For example, one page of simple text with no fancy formatting or graphics typically comprises at least 24,000 bits, or 3,000 bytes, of information. At a nominal 2,400 bps, a slow but still common modem speed, it takes at least 11 seconds to transfer each page of text. Text that must be transmitted with specific fonts or formatting, or in word processor or spreadsheet format, requires a somewhat larger number of bits depending on the features and formats that are included. A 1-megabyte file takes more than 1 hour to transfer at 2,400 bps but only a few seconds over a very lightly loaded network running at 10 megabits per second (Mbps). Depending on the resolution and number of shades of gray required, a one-page, black-and-white graphic image comprises between 1 and 4 megabytes.

Bandwidth is even more critical for media that must be transmitted in an ongoing data stream such as audio or video. One second of telephone-quality audio requires approximately 64,000 bits. Full-color, full-motion video conforming to regular U.S. television standards (as set forth by the National Television Systems Committee) requires a bandwidth of 180 Mbps. These numbers can be reduced by limiting the resolution of the image, transmitting fewer frames per second, and utilizing various compression algorithms. However, bandwidths on the order of 1.5 Mbps to 8 Mbps are still required to achieve reasonable quality. From these considerations, it is easy to see that video applications are far more demanding than audio applications, which are in turn more demanding than still-image and text-only applications.

Envisioning the Applications Enabled by Unlimited Bandwidth

The introduction of microprocessors and their rapid penetration of the market have resulted in a drastic reduction in the cost of computer processing cycles. The National Information Infrastructure (NII) will have a similar effect on the cost of communications: it will make long-haul, high-bandwidth connections less expensive and more widely available. However, lower-bandwidth cellular and wireless technologies will also become widely available, and low-bandwidth, analog telephone lines will continue to be used in many homes and sparsely populated areas. Thus, distributed work applications utilizing the NII will need to be integrated well across different network technologies and bandwidths. Important research areas will include system infrastructure, user interfaces, and developing applications that will effectively use the varying bandwidths available.

For example, the processor, the internal data communications bus, and the input/output systems of desktop computers are now very powerful, with further increases coming at a rapid rate. How could high network bandwidth and abundant, inexpensive desktop computing power be combined and integrated to enable, for example, useful and innovative distance learning applications to improve education? Some possibilities, with widely differing bandwidth requirements, might include the following:

• Dynamically creating a single video data stream with the "audience" incorporated into the image. This would allow, for example, each participant in a distributed industrial or professional training session to pan and zoom within the videoconference or presentation just as he or she might look back and forth between the presenter and the other participants in a small workshop or seminar;
• Dynamically analyzing the facial expressions of the audience to create different measures and displays summarizing audience response (e.g., 30 percent of the audience shows evidence of understanding what is being presented);

• Capturing and organizing audio questions from audience members during the lecture that can be reviewed and/or responded to by the lecturer later. In other words, members of the audience can create private audio messages that are passed to the lecturer;

• Capturing and indexing the lecture so that members of the audience can more easily locate and review what the lecturer said;

• Providing audience members access to the source material on which the lecture is based so that they can browse through it during the lecture; and

• Broadcasting several video streams and allowing audience members to select among them or to watch several at the same time.

Similar possibilities exist for other applications. The key idea is to determine how bandwidth could be used if it were effectively unconstrained, so as to better understand its usefulness for distributed work.

Enabling Integration of Low- and High-Bandwidth Applications

At the same time, bandwidth limitations will exist for traditional telephone service, wireless connections, and cellular services for a long time. Thus, applications and devices that can provide essential functions using limited bandwidth and yet be integrated well with devices and services provided over high-bandwidth networks also should be developed. One example might be to allow a person to cooperate in a videoconference using a personal digital assistant (PDA) with limited computational power. While the video portion would likely be a casualty of limited bandwidth, the audio channel could be played and a shared drawing browser could be used in a discussion between a field repair person and a technical support desk. The audio channel might be sent over a cellular network, and the shared drawing tool commands might be sent over the PDA wireless network. More generally, communications protocols that have little overhead and that can utilize processing power to substitute for bandwidth are fertile areas for further technical research.

MEETING REQUIREMENTS FOR MULTIMEDIA COMMUNICATION

The distributed work environments of the future will clearly involve the transmission and reception of multiple types of communications traffic, including voice, data images, video, and data files. Multimedia communication is particularly demanding because video and audio data must generally arrive in real time, although delays may be tolerated in the receipt of data files and images. The objective, in the general sense, is to enable people to engage in multimedia communications independent of location, distance, computing and communications environment, or the number of parties involved in a given collaborative session.

User Requirements

The type of distributed work session might range from that involving a single individual carrying a wireless-network computer interacting with a remote database to a large-scale multimedia teleconference or group work session involving many remotely located parties as well as specialized servers for video, image, and data. Individuals in such a multimedia, multiparty conference or work session must be free to come and go. Subconferences might be convened and later, the full session reconvened. Different types of media might be transmitted to all or subsets of the group at any given time.

Participants in a distributed work environment do not want to be aware of the underlying communications infrastructure required to make their sessions or conferences possible. They want to turn on intelligent systems, indicate with whom they wish to communicate, and start the session within, almost literally, the blink of an eyelid. They want the chance of a session setup being denied due to lack of network resources to be as small as it is currently for voice telephone calls—about 1 percent or less. While users may recognize that video, voice, and images in a wireless environment may not be received with the same fidelity as in the wired environment, the quality of service clearly has to be acceptable no matter where users are located and how they move.

Quality-of-service requirements vary greatly, depending on the type of data being transferred. For example, computer data files must be transferred without loss or corruption but can generally be delayed during transmission. Real-time voice, on the other hand, is recognizable in spite of some loss or corruption during transmission, but substantial loss or delay results in unacceptable degradation. The delay and loss requirements for real-time video over communication networks are not completely understood at this time and depend on the kind of compression techniques used in transmitting the video and on the quality of image that is required. A multimedia, multipoint network must ensure that the different media arrive in reasonable synchronism at any given receiver site and appear at nearly the same time at the different sites.

As an example, consider a three-party work session with users located in New York City, Boston, and Honolulu. The New York user sends a multimedia message involving video with audio, a number of images, and some accompanying data, with each medium to be displayed on a different window on the recipients' screens. Four different kinds of media are involved. Assume that the transmission to Hawaii encounters a network problem resulting in some loss of data. The lost data are repeated a number of times before finally arriving correctly at their destination. The video and its accompanying audio information are separated from each other and from the data, following different paths because of differing bandwidth requirements. How will the audio and video be appropriately resynchronized at the two receiving workstations, and how will the system and/or users handle latency problems resulting from the fact that the complete, correct multimedia data took longer to reach Hawaii than Boston? Issues such as these must be addressed in the context of research into multimedia, multipoint protocols.

Technology Requirements

At least three enabling technologies are required for effective multimedia communication among users distributed in time and space.

1. A high-speed, broadband, wired communications infrastructure to handle diverse multimedia traffic;
2. A wireless networking environment capable of handling multimedia traffic; and
3. Multimedia communication protocols appropriate over wide areas and involving multiple parties in heterogeneous computing environments, i.e., multimedia, multiparty protocols.

Multimedia, multiparty communications capability is already available to a limited extent over local area networks and is clearly a topic of great interest among computer, workstation, and communications vendors. Multimedia communication over wide areas is still in its infancy, with many research issues yet to be addressed. A limited amount of multimedia protocol design for the Internet has been carried out. Some work on point-to-point multimedia communication protocols, as contrasted to multiparty communications (group work sessions and teleconferences), has appeared in the technical literature. However, the bulk of the work carried out thus far on multimedia communications has focused on workstation design and issues such as the synchronization of different traffic types. In the terminology of network communications architecture, research attention has been focused principally on the "higher-layer" protocols. Relatively little work has been carried out on the communications infrastructure, including the transport layer, required for long-distance multimedia communications over wide area networks. The recently published *Realizing the Information Future* (CSTB, 1994b) has called for an expanded program of research to support an Open Data Network architecture that would facilitate multimedia traffic.

5

Research Recommendations

Distributed work, including telecommuting, relies heavily on computing and communications technologies. Recent improvements in the capabilities and availability of tools in these interrelated fields have meant that distributed work can be undertaken more easily now than in the past. Likewise, future improvements will benefit those engaging in distributed work and provide both economic and social benefits to the nation. Thus the committee supports the continuation of broad national computing and communications research programs in academia, industry, and government.

However, in order to optimize the opportunities for and effectiveness of distributed work, the committee recommends that research also be conducted with distributed work as a specific focus. The research needed can be conceptualized as indicated in Figure 5.1: infrastructure research is most needed at the extremes of the range of computing and communications capabilities, and applications research is most needed in the middle of the spectrum.

INFRASTRUCTURE RESEARCH

The national initiative to develop the technologies for and establish the National Information Infrastructure (NII) will benefit distributed work. For example, the NII will require both richer and more robust security features than are now available on the Internet. These

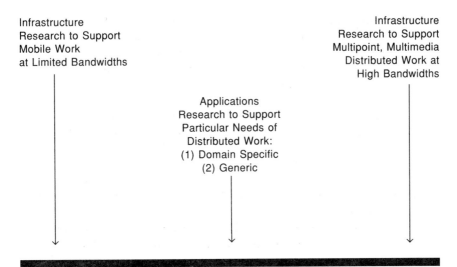

Infrastructure
Research to Support
Mobile Work
at Limited Bandwidths

Infrastructure
Research to Support
Multipoint, Multimedia
Distributed Work at
High Bandwidths

Applications
Research to Support
Particular Needs of
Distributed Work:
(1) Domain Specific
(2) Generic

Computing and Communications Capabilities

FIGURE 5.1 Types of research needed to support distributed work across a range of capabilities.

same features will of course be useful to distributed workers to help ensure proper access, control, authentication, and tracking of both individual and group work. The committee recommends that specific technical infrastructure research to enhance and extend distributed work practices be undertaken in the following areas.

Mobile Work

Working while mobile, for example, while traveling in a automobile or standing in a customer's office, presents many challenges due to the limited communications bandwidth and computing power that are typically available compared to those offered in a stationary environment with wire or optical fiber network connections. While pocket-size cellular telephones have enabled voice communications for many users, reliable mobile data communications services are just now being deployed and are still typically limited to asynchronous, low-bandwidth applications like electronic mail or its equivalent. Similarly, computing power becomes limited as equipment size and weight are restricted. Laptop computers, weighing a few pounds and suitable for use while sitting down, are capable of running most programs from a desktop computer environment, but computing power and thus the programs that can be used become extremely constrained on a "palm-top" device suitable for use while standing or walking.

To help increase the usefulness of mobile devices and services, the committee recommends a comprehensive research program with the following major elements (goals):

- Increasing the bandwidth available to mobile devices. This might include using multiple channels or transmission technologies to increase the effective delivered bandwidth.
- Developing network protocols that specifically facilitate mobile addresses or end-points. (The current protocols, TCP/IP and ISO TP4, were developed under the assumption of geographically fixed end-points.)
- Effectively and efficiently allocating among multiple media (e.g., image, text, audio, and signaling) the varying bandwidth that is available to a mobile user. Both short-term variances caused by circumstances such as changes in network load and long-term variances attributable to advances in transmission technology will need to be gracefully accommodated with minimal user attention.
- Balancing and accommodating the competing service demands and network traffic generated by multiple, simultaneous mobile users.
- Maintaining the essential functionality of communications that originate in a high-bandwidth environment but must be delivered in environments of varying bandwidth, including those of low-bandwidth mobile devices.
- Managing the real-time tracking and transfer of users moving between wireless cells, and ultimately the transfer of users moving from a wired to a wireless network environment in the course of a single, multimedia work or conference session.[1]
- Developing computer processes and programs that can migrate across a network with the user as that individual moves from place to place. (Ubiquitous computing and a mobile computing environment are similar concepts.)
- Facilitating periods of "disconnected work" done when a network connection is not available. Currently, even the best-connected

---

[1]Wireless systems already track users in order to provide uninterrupted service. However, safeguards must be established to prevent the system from being abused as a way to simply monitor the movements of citizens for other reasons. This is one concrete example of the need for implementing privacy safeguards as the nation's technology advances.

mobile workers have some periods when they must work with no network connection at all, such as during commercial air flights. This can present a problem when their work involves files that are shared with other workers: when a temporarily disconnected worker returns to connected operations, how can he or she know which version of each file is the latest, and how can the changes made by the temporarily disconnected worker be reconciled with a file that may also have been changed by workers within the group who remained connected?

Complicating but also adding promise in low-bandwidth-environment research is the fact that computing power and communications bandwidth can often be substituted, one for the other. For example, if a suitable processor and algorithm are available, data compression can reduce the need for large bandwidths by effectively decreasing the quantity of information that must be transmitted.

Multipoint, Multimedia Distributed Work

A broad-ranging technical research program should be initiated to explore possibilities for distributed work practices using multipoint, multimedia communications at different, but generally abundant, bandwidths.[2] In addition to facilitating distributed work, a research program in this area would help ensure the timely implementation of the NII. It should include research aimed at achieving the following:

• Understanding and specifying minimum quality-of-service standards for a representative variety of application areas. Currently, the impacts of conditions such as latency, jitter, buffering, and synchronization of high-quality, interactive audio, image, and video are not fully understood. For example, the amount of video jitter that is acceptable for distance learning may be figuratively and literally deadly in a telemedicine application. The requirements for latency, jitter, and the like may also differ between live and delayed (recorded) viewing.

---

[2]Related sociological, organizational, and human-factors research will need to be conducted contemporaneously with technical research. For example, videoconferencing is still a relatively new technique: we use it, but not necessarily well. How can it be made more effective? What formats are good for meetings? How can both previously prepared and spontaneously written materials best be integrated into a videoconference?

- Predicting and controlling the various types of simultaneous communications traffic to ensure the required quality of services for both point-to-point and multipoint sessions. This may involve individuals using devices with varying bandwidth capabilities joining and leaving during an active session.

- Determining how to charge for distributed patterns of resource consumption on complex networks that may include sections of varying bandwidth. For example, the current conference-call model of charging a single party with the entire cost of a distributed work session is very likely to inhibit usage when newer, more complex networks and connections are available and are used by multiple organizations that have agreed to be responsible for their own costs while cooperating on a particular project. Specifically, a party participating via a limited-bandwidth connection in an otherwise high-bandwidth, multimedia, six-way conference session may not wish to pay one-sixth of the total cost of the session. Ideally, a variety of methods for billing according to bandwidth use or allocation should be supported.

- Establishing multimedia communication sessions among multiple, remote parties, to include notification of individuals and initiation of the actual session with minimal human attention.

APPLICATIONS RESEARCH

Domain-Specific Research

Although various types of distributed work are currently carried out in the U.S. workplace, the implementation and effectiveness of important organizational group processes are often constrained by the lack of relevant computing and communications applications in a distributed work environment. For example, the informal methods that people in organizations have for sharing information, coordinating tasks, learning new skills, recruiting members, and sustaining group activities cannot be applied easily in distributed settings. The committee believes that many of these processes can be facilitated by a sustained research effort focusing on computing and communications applications for distributed work.

Thus, the committee recommends research-oriented field trials of distributed work in areas of national or commercial interest, such as delivery of health care in rural areas, collaborative design of complex systems, or the maintenance and repair of deployed equipment. These trials should be conducted across large geographic areas and should utilize heterogeneous hardware, software, and communications services whenever possible. As appropriate, they could be combined with other federal and state field trials of distributed education, health care, distributed science, or electronic commerce. The field trials should lead to the development of applications tailored to improve performance in each of these domains. Importantly, it appears that with minor modifications they will enhance distributed work in other domains as well. The committee believes that similar efforts in other important areas of distributed work would help solve the difficult problems of information sharing, group socialization, remote supervision, and related constraints in the context of employer-employee relationships. Properly designed field trials of distributed work would provide the opportunity to conduct extensive research in important substantive areas such as education and on tools such as group writing products that could enhance and extend future distributed work in many other fields or domains. Research should be conducted to discover approaches to the following:

- Improving the capability to search for and share unstructured information. Research aimed at improving the tools needed to identify potential group members and to identify and access personal stores of information in the same manner as information stored in libraries and other institutional archives is only starting, and more is clearly needed. Even if the technological problem of finding experts were solved, the social issues of ensuring privacy and controlling access to expert individuals across networks need extensive research. Numerous opportunities for research also exist in the area of search algorithms capable of handling nonstandardized information formats on heterogeneous hardware platforms.

- Developing techniques for forming and sustaining distributed groups, including methods for developing group cohesiveness, enabling remote supervision, providing individual and group motivation and rewards, and ensuring continued commitment to a project or organization. Behavioral and organizational research should be conducted concurrently to better identify exactly how physical proximity stimulates effective recruitment of group members, so that functionally analogous processes can be encouraged in distributed work settings.

- Scaling and extending information retrieval techniques so that users can search all relevant and available databases, not just previously known and selected databases. Query techniques that are independent of the underlying database structure will be increasingly valuable as increasing amounts of information become accessible via public networks such as the Internet. Related research is needed into highly reliable global file systems and environments and on improving the performance of distributed databases, and their impacts on network traffic. More generally, research is needed to develop techniques for browsing and other ways of facilitating queries in which the user may not have a well-specified question.

•   Developing portable, extensible tool kits for building distributed remote control systems and their user interfaces. For example, key control functions must be identified and made accessible to remote control, security and safety must be foolproof, and both novice and expert users must be accommodated. Additionally, researchers should investigate the potentials for controlling heterogeneous devices with the same end functions through a single remote control program.

The field trials recommended by the committee should be interdisciplinary research efforts, with expert personnel drawn from the behavioral and social sciences as well as from the computing and telecommunications disciplines. Social and behavioral scientists have extensive understanding of the functions that groups need to fulfill to successfully accomplish their work and experience in evaluating the success with which new computer and communications-based tools have met these needs, as well as expertise in assessing the social impact of new tools and technologies. Technology researchers have expertise in inventing successful applications that push the limits of technology, that can be generalized across domains, and that raise fundamental research issues in the supporting technical disciplines. Together they can explore the interrelated technical, human, organizational, and social factors that can enhance and extend distributed work across many discipline- and situation-specific domains.

Generic Research

Computers have provided powerful new capabilities to the nation's workers. Word processors and desktop publishing programs make writing, editing, laying out, designing, and publishing sophisticated documents dependent on the skill of the individual rather than on the availability of expensive specialized equipment. Spreadsheet and graphics programs allow legions of workers to analyze scientific, financial, and other numerical data in sophisticated ways that prior to 1980 were possible only for those with access to large mainframe computers. Database programs allow workers with only minimal programming skills to record, store, retrieve, and analyze huge amounts of data.

However, with these ever-increasing capabilities has come increasing complexity. Workers needing to cooperate with others must now be conversant about multiple file formats and their compatibility (or general lack thereof), translation utilities, diskette formats, data densities, and even features supported between versions or releases of the same program. While these intricacies are reasonably manageable within a single, physically contiguous organization with ample technical support, they can quickly become very limiting within a geographically distributed work group using heterogeneous hardware, software, and communications media. Mobile workers may have an even more difficult time as they attempt to communicate and cooperate across time zones utilizing unfamiliar telephone and data connections with little or no technical support.

If the capacity for distributed work is to expand to individuals and groups beyond those with considerable technical proficiency, attention must be paid to simplifying many of the required operations and user interfaces. The committee thus recommends a research program with the following goals:

• Developing distributed work tools, interfaces, and systems that actively encourage information sharing. This activity is critical to group accomplishments and can become difficult in dispersed groups. New systems should include features to anticipate and accommodate work conditions described in the social science literature—such as social dilemmas, social loafing, and altruism—to improve information sharing.

• Bridging the gap between synchronous and asynchronous communications to facilitate both prior input and follow-up to group work sessions. Currently, distributed group discussions and work sessions tend to take place synchronously, using only a few specifically preannounced reference or discussion items. Extensive pre- and post-session discussions occurring by asynchronous means such as electronic mail are often ignored or imperfectly summarized and considered due to the difficulties of indexing, referencing, conveniently using, and generally relating them to a work session occurring on a synchronous medium. Technical and human-factors research may reveal methods to better link these two major categories of communication.

• Improving and extending the user interface to the telephone network and services. The nearly universal 12-key touch-tone keypad has become a limiting factor in many systems. So-called voice response systems use audio only on one end of the transaction, and users must be led through a long menu tree in order to limit the number of choices at any one branch. Interfaces might be both richer and easier to use with some combination of alphanumeric display, voice prompts, and audio input from the user. Even in an age of growing computer networks, "plain old telephone service" remains the most ubiquitous means of sharing information.

• Improving audio processing technology and equipment to facilitate working at a distance. This effort should include research aimed at better managing and using captured audio as a data type, and improving noise and echo cancellation in less-than-ideal audio environments.

• Reducing the human support currently needed for the use of widespread, complex networks by distributed workers. Currently, wide area network services, whether provided directly through Internet connections or indirectly by value-added network vendors, generally require large amounts of human-provided technical support. This is especially true when end users do not wish to learn about underlying network technologies. Research aimed at better automating long- and short-term network connections as well as ongoing network trouble-shooting and maintenance would be valuable to all individuals engaging in distributed work and to most other network users as well.

• Improving the quality and reducing the cost of powerful, high-quality computer input and output devices. While these improvements would aid all workers, distributed workers in particular must often process large amounts of information with little support from others. Improved scanning, optical character recognition, and computer display systems would be very helpful. Better interfaces are needed for browsing, annotating, retaining, and communicating the context of information.

• Improving the reliability of communications and computing systems to reduce the chance of telecommuters becoming isolated due to system failures. Networks and multiuser systems of all types will need to have the same or better reliability as today's stand-alone, single-user systems.

CONCLUSION

Many observers believe that the U.S. economy is in transition to a postindustrial model. While the exact outlines of this new economy are not yet completely known, it appears that the nation would be well served by enhancing workers' capabilities to engage in distributed work and by carefully considering its wider adoption in order to increase locational flexibility, provide expanded employment opportunities, and make better use of our physical transportation resources. The research recommendations of the Committee to Study

Technology and Telecommuting: Issues and Impacts will by no means be the final word on the topic. New opportunities for research will appear as the nation's work practices change and its computing and communications technology continues to advance. The committee is convinced, however, that the research it has recommended will provide major new technological capabilities to enhance and extend the use of distributed work in the nation.

Bibliography

Abel, M.J. 1990. "Experiences in an exploratory distributed organization." Pp. 489-510 in J. Galegher, R. Kraut, and C. Egido, eds., *Intellectual Teamwork: Social and Technological Foundations of Cooperative Work.* Hillsdale, N.J.: Lawrence Earlbaum Associates.

Allen, T. 1977. *Managing the Flow of Technology.* Cambridge, Mass: MIT Press.

Argote, L. 1982. "Input uncertainty and organizational coordination in hospital emergency units." *Administrative Science Quarterly* 27:420-434.

Bagley, M., J. Mannering, and P. Mokhtarian. 1993. *Telecommuting Centers and Related Concepts: A Review of Practice.* University of California, Davis, Institute of Transportation Studies Research Report, prepared for the California Department of Transportation Office of Traffic Improvement (December).

Baiylin, L. 1988. *Toward the Perfect Workplace? The Experience of Home-based Developers.* Working paper 1993-88. Cambridge, Mass.: Sloan School of Management, Massachusetts Institute of Technology.

Bly, S., S. Harrison, and S. Irwin. 1993. "Media spaces: Bringing people together in a video, audio and computing environment." *Communications of the ACM* 36(1):28-46.

Borenstein, N. 1992. "Computational mail as network infrastructure for CSCW." *Proceedings of Computer Supported Cooperative Work 1992.* New York: Association of Computing Machinery.

Brooks, F. 1975. *The Mythical Man-month: Essays on Software Engineering*. Reading, Mass.: Addison-Wesley Publishing Company.

Bullen, C., and J. Bennett. 1991. "Groupware in practice. An interpretation of work experiences." Pp. 257-287 in C. Dunlop and R. Kling, eds., *Computerization and Controversy: Value Conflicts and Social Choices*. New York: Academic Press.

Christensen, K. 1988. *Women and Home-Based Work: The Unspoken Contract*. New York: Henry Holt and Company.

Clark, H.H., and S.E. Brennen. 1991. "Grounding in communication." Pp. 127-149 in L.B. Resnick, R.M. Levine, and S.D. Teasley, eds., *Perspectives on Socially Shared Cognition*. Washington, D.C.: American Psychological Association.

Computer Science and Technology Board (CSTB), National Research Council. 1990. *Computers at Risk: Safe Computing in the Information Age*. Washington, D.C.: National Academy Press.

Computer Science and Telecommunications Board (CSTB), National Research Council. 1993. *National Collaboratories: Applying Information Technology for Scientific Research*. Washington, D.C.: National Academy Press.

Computer Science and Telecommunications Board (CSTB), National Research Council. 1994a. *Information Technology in the Service Society: A Twenty-First Century Lever*. Washington, D.C.: National Academy Press.

Computer Science and Telecommunications Board (CSTB), National Research Council. 1994b. *Realizing the Information Future: The Internet and Beyond*. Washington, D.C.: National Academy Press.

Computer Science and Telecommunications Board (CSTB), National Research Council. 1994c. *Rights and Responsibilities of Participants in Networked Communities*. Washington, D.C.: National Academy Press, in press.

Constant, D., L. Sproull, and S. Kiesler. 1994. "The kindness of strangers: On the usefulness of weak ties for technical advice." *Organizational Science*, forthcoming.

Culnan, M. 1983. "Environmental scanning: The effects of task complexity and source accessibility on information gathering behavior." *Decision Science* 14:194-206.

de Sola Pool, I. 1980. "Communications technology and land use." *Annals of the American Academy of Political and Social Science* 451(September):1-12.

Dudley, K., R. Kraut, and C. Steinfield. 1993. *American Home Telecommunications Project*. Unpublished research. Morristown, N.J.: Bell Communications Research.

Eveland, J., and T. Bikson. 1988. "Work group structures and computer support: A field experiment." *ACM Transactions on Office Information Systems* 6(4):354-379.

Feldman, M.S. 1987. "Electronic mail and weak ties in organizations." *Office: Technology and People* 3:83-101.

Festinger, L., S. Schacter, and K. Back. 1950. *Social Pressures in Informal Groups: A Study of Human Factors in Housing.* Palo Alto, Calif.: Stanford University Press.

Finholt, T., and C. Huff. 1994. *Social Issues in Computing: Putting Computing in Its Place.* New York: McGraw-Hill.

Fish, R., R. Kraut, R. Root, and R. Rice. 1992. "Evaluating video as a technology for informal communication." *Communications of the ACM* 36(1):48-61.

Flores, F., M. Graves, B. Hartfield, and T. Winograd. 1988. "Computer systems and the design of organizational interaction." *ACM Transactions on Office Information Systems* 6:153-172.

Foltz, P., and S. Dumais. 1993. "Personalized information delivery: An analysis of information filtering methods." *Communications of the ACM* 35(12):51-60.

Galegher, J., and R. Kraut. 1994. "Computer-mediated communication for intellectual teamwork: An experiment in group writing." *Information Systems Research* 5(2):110-138.

Garvey, W., N. Lin, and C. Nelson. 1970. "Communication in the physical and social sciences." *Science* 170:1166-1173.

Gentile, F., and R. Houseman. 1970. *A Development Project in Self and Home Employment for the Homebound.* Albertson, N.Y.: INA Mend Institute at Human Resources Center.

Gibbons, J., W. Kincheloe, and K. Down. 1977. "Tutored videotape instruction." *Science* 195:1139.

Hagstrom, W. 1965. *The Scientific Community.* Carbondale, Ill.: Southern Illinois University Press, pp. 121-122.

Hesses, B., L. Sproull, S. Kiesler, and J. Walsh. 1993. "Returns to science: Computer networks and scientific research in oceanography." *Communications of the ACM* 36(8):90-101.

Hiltz, S. 1993. "Correlates of learning in a virtual classroom." *International Journal of Man-Machine Studies* 39:71-98.

Ives, H. 1930. "Two-way television." *Bell Labs Record* 8:399-404.

Katz, D., and R. Kahn. 1979. *The Social Psychology of Organizations.* Second edition. New York: John Wiley & Sons.

Katz, R., and M. Tushman. 1978. "Communication patterns, project performance, and task characteristics: An empirical evaluation in an R&D setting." *Organizational Behavior and Human Performance* 23:139-162.

Kraut, R. 1988. "Homework: What is it and who does it?" Chapter

2 in K. Christensen, ed., *The New Era of Home-based Work.* Boulder, Colo.: Westview Press.

Kraut, R., and P. Attewell. 1993. *Electronic Mail and Organizational Knowledge: Media Use in a Global Corporation.* Technical Report CMU-CS-93-208. Pittsburgh, Pa.: Carnegie Mellon University, Computer Science Department.

Kraut, R., and L. Streeter. 1994. "Coordination in large scale software development." *Communications of the ACM,* in press.

Kraut, R., C. Egido, and J. Galegher. 1990. "Patterns of contact and communication in scientific research collaboration." Pp. 149-171 in J. Galegher, R. Kraut, and C. Egido, eds., *Intellectual Teamwork: Social and Technological Foundations of Cooperative Work.* Hillsdale, N.J.: Lawrence Erlbaum Associates.

Kraut, R., S. Lewis, and L. Swezey. 1982. "Listener responsiveness and the coordination of conversation." *Journal of Personality and Social Psychology* 43:718-731.

Kusterer, K. 1978. *Know-how on the Job: The Important Working Knowledge of Unskilled Workers.* Boulder, Colo.: Westview Press.

Lai, K., T. Malone, and K. Yu. 1988. "Object lens: A "spreadsheet" for cooperative work." *ACM Transactions on Office Information Systems* 6(4):332-353.

LaRose, R. 1983. *Future Demand for Teleconferencing and Teleconferencing Suppliers.* East Lansing, Mich.: EELRA Group.

Lave, J., and E. Wenger. 1991. *Situated Learning: Legitimate Peripheral Participation.* New York: Cambridge University Press.

Lund, J., and P. Mokhtarian. 1994. "Telecommuting and residential location: Theory and implications for VMT in the monocentric metropolis." *Transportation Research Record,* forthcoming.

McGraw-Hill Encyclopedia of Science & Technology. 1987. "Facsimile." Sixth edition. New York: McGraw-Hill.

Miller, J., M. McKenna, and P. Ramsey. 1993. "An evaluation of student content learning and affective perceptions of a two-way interactive video learning experience." *Educational Technology* 33(6):51-55.

Mintzberg, H. 1979. *The Structuring of Organizations.* Englewood Cliffs, N.J.: Prentice-Hall, p. 20.

Mokhtarian, P. 1988. "An empirical evaluation of the travel impacts of teleconferencing." *Transportation Research A* 22A(4):283-289.

Mokhtarian, P. 1990. "A typology of relationships between telecommunications and transportation." *Transportation Research A* 24A(3):231-242.

Mokhtarian, P. 1991a. "Defining telecommuting." *Transportation Research Record* 1305:273-281.

Mokhtarian, P. 1991b. "Telecommuting and travel: State of the practice, state of the art." *Transportation* 18(4):319-342.

Mokhtarian, P. 1994. "The transportation impacts of telecommuting: Recent empirical findings." In P.R. Stopher and M. Lee-Gosselin, eds., *Understanding Travel Behavior in an Era of Change.* Elmsford, N.Y.: Pergamon Press, forthcoming.

Mokhtarian, P., and I. Salomon. 1994. "Modeling the choice of telecommuting: Setting the context." *Environment and Planning A* 26(4):749-766.

Mokhtarian, P., S. Handy, and I. Salomon. 1994. "Methodological issues in the estimation of transportation, energy, and air quality impacts of telecommuting." *Transportation Research A,* forthcoming.

National Technological University (NTU). 1994. "National Technological University: Press fact sheet." NTU, 700 Centre Ave., Fort Collins, Colo., August.

Nijkamp, P., and I. Salomon. 1989. "Future spatial impacts of telecommunications." *Transportation Planning and Technology* 13(4):275-287.

Nilles, J. 1991. "Telecommuting and urban sprawl: Mitigator or inciter?" *Transportation* 18(4):411-432.

Ochsman, R., and A. Chapanis. 1974. "The effects of 10 communications modes on the behavior of teams during co-operative problem solving." *International Journal of Man-Machine Studies* 6(September):579-619.

O'Conaill, B., S. Whittaker, and S. Wilbur. 1992. *Conversations over video-conferences: An evaluation of video mediated communication.* Unpublished manuscript. Bristol, England: Hewlett Packard Research Laboratories.

Race, T. 1993. "Testing the telecommute." *New York Times,* August 6, p. F11.

Salomon, I. 1986. "Telecommuting and travel relationships: A review." *Transportation Research A* 20(3):223-238.

Salton, G., and M. McGill. 1979. *Introduction to Modern Information Retrieval.* New York: McGraw-Hill Books.

Schramm, W. 1977. *Big Media, Little Media: Tools and Technologies for Instruction.* Beverly Hills, Calif.: Sage Publications.

Shellenbarger, S. 1993. "Some thrive, but many wilt working at home." *Wall Street Journal,* December 14, p. B1.

Smailagic, A., and D. Siewiorek. 1994. "The CMU mobile computers." *Proceedings of IEEE COMPCON '94.* New York: Institute of Electrical and Electronics Engineers.

Svenning, L., and J. Ruchinskas. 1984. "Organizational teleconferencing." Pp. 217-248 in Ronald E. Rice Associates, eds., *The New Media*. Beverly Hills, Calif.: Sage Publications.

Tang, J., and E. Isaacs. 1992. *Why Do Users Like Video? Studies of Multimedia-supported Collaboration*. SMLI TR-92-5. Mountain View, Calif.: Sun Microsystems Laboratories.

Thorn, B., and T. Connolly. 1987. "Discretionary data bases: A theory and some experimental findings." *Communications Research* 14(5):512-528.

Tushman, M. 1977. "Special boundary roles in the innovation process." *Administrative Science Quarterly* 22(4):587-605.

U.S. Department of Energy. 1994. *Energy, Emissions, and Social Consequences of Telecommuting*. Washington, D.C.: U.S. Government Printing Office.

U.S. Department of Labor. 1991. *Dictionary of Occupational Titles*. Volume 1. Fourth edition. Lanham, Md.: Bernan Press.

U.S. Department of Transportation, Office of the Secretary. 1993. *Transportation Implications of Telecommuting*. Washington, D.C.: U.S. Government Printing Office.

Weiser, M. 1993. "Some computer science issues in ubiquitous computing." *Communications of the ACM* 36(7):47-84.

Whitaker, S., and E. Geelhoed. 1993. "Shared workspaces. How do they work and when are they useful?" *International Journal of Man-Machine Studies* 39:813-842.

Williams, E. 1977. "Experimental comparisons of face-to-face and mediated communication: A review." *Psychological Bulletin* 84:963-976.

Yates, J. 1989. *Control Through Communication*. Baltimore, Md.: Johns Hopkins University Press.